Case Studies in Business Planning

CW01064746

Case Studies in Business Planning

Bill Richardson · Glyn Owen
John Patterson · Peter Jennings
Business Policy Team, Sheffield City Polytechnic

Pitman

PITMAN PUBLISHING
128 Long Acre, London WC2E 9AN
A Division of Longman Group UK Limited

© Longman Group UK Ltd 1989

First published in Great Britain 1989

British Library Cataloguing in Publication Data

Richardson, Bill
  Case studies in Business planning:
  1. Business firms. Planning
  I. Title
  658.4'012

ISBN 0 273 03127 9

Set in Linotron 202 10/12pt Times Roman

Printed in Great Britain at The Bath Press, Avon

Contents

---

* Sample topics covered – NB: Almost all the cases lend themselves to
   a consideration of environmental change and the changing nature of
   environments.

   The case studies in this book are intended to be aids to student
learning rather than comments on the handling.of particular business
situations.

Preface

Plans and decisions are the vital prerequisites to the actual work performed by organisations. Business success depends upon successful planning and decision-making. The organisation itself is a strategy for the attainment of desired futures – for all those who interact with it. All those plans and decisions, which the organisation undertakes and implements, together contribute to the success of the organisation as a strategy.

At the heart of university, polytechnic and college business studies/organisation studies type courses and subjects, is the quest to improve students' planning/decision-making skills. This underlying aim applies across the full range of diploma, certificate, degree and postgraduate courses and to all students – whether full time, part time, in or out of employment. Increasingly practising managers are looking for help towards the improvement of their decision-making skills.

At Sheffield we view Strategy (with a capital 'S') as the organisation itself – a mechanism for creating wealth and offering satisfactions to people who interact with it. The successful organisation breeds wealth and satisfies aspirations as it moves through its environments over time. *All* the plans, decisions and activities made and implemented by the organisation impact on the levels of strategic success achieved, ie Strategy making is much more than the making of those major product/market choices and implementations which form the subject-matter of many corporate strategy type programmes of study. This book and its sister publication, *Business Planning: An Approach to Strategic Management*, are intended to help improve skills across the range of organisational planning activities.

At Sheffield Polytechnic, our Business/Management Studies courses are built around central modules of study which consider specifically management strategy issues. (Management strategy, in this context, is that field of study concerned with the management of the total organisation, with particular emphasis on its decisional behaviour.) A 'spine' for the BA Business Studies programme, for example, is created by our Business Functions, Business Environment, Business Decision-Making and Business Policy modules. These modules, in the chronological order set out above, also provide links throughout the life of the course. Other Sheffield programmes are structured similarly. Other institutions, we know, offer broadly similar programme structures. This book is intended for use with these central decision-making units. It is a book containing case studies which can be used across the range of decision-making subjects through the life of student programmes of business studies.

For practitioners of business this book provides models of business problems, and approaches to business problems, which provides vehicles for learning how more customised plans and decisions might be better made.

A case is a written description of an organisation. The primary reasons for using a case study for business education are to enable the student to see how actual organisations have performed the strategic management process and to allow students to practice and develop their skills in applying strategic management concepts to actual organisations. The cases in this book have already been used at Sheffield for this purpose. They have been created from material taken from real organisations. While in some instances the identities of these organisations have been disguised, nevertheless, students should be aware that the problems addressed in the case studies *are* real. We hope that this one book encapsulates enough 'real' organisational problems and activities to provide a continuous source of fruitful material – to assist in the study of organisation planning and decision-making throughout the life of the students' decision-making studies.

This book has a sister text *Business Planning: An Approach to Strategic Management* W Richardson & R Richardson, Pitman Publishing, 1989, which can be used to advantage as a complementary medium for the teaching and learning of strategic planning.

Acknowledgements are due to colleagues who have provided material for this book and who are identified in the contents pages. Special thanks is due to Maurice Brown, Ian King, Janet Kirkham, Sue Leeson, Dick Gadsden, David Holmes, Nick Foster, Graham Worsdale, Ken Roberts, Marie-Ann Rijs and Annie Robinson who have helped test and improve the material. Last but not least, we offer our thanks to students, past and present for their contributions to this book and to our personal development.

Bill Richardson
Glyn Owen
John Patterson
Peter Jennings

Members of the Business Policy Team,
Sheffield City Polytechnic

1 · Medway Menswear Ltd

Bill Richardson and Mary Klemm

This case study has been written by Bill Richardson from general experience. It is intended as an aid to class discussion rather than as a comment on the handling of a business situation. (Amendments by Mary Klemm.) It is presented in the form of an interview between Derek Armitage, Managing Director of Medway Menswear and Polytechnic Consultants.

'The best time to change is when you are doing well! The best time to spend money on changing is when you've got some. If you wait until you are forced to change it's often already too late. It nearly was too late for us, but I think we've managed to turn the tide.'

Derek Armitage got up from his chair, and tidied the papers on his desk.

'Our present position owes much to hard work, effort and co-operation on everybody's part – directors, management and staff throughout the organisation. I'm also aware, however, that we've been lucky. We were in the right place at the right time – as much by chance as by design – and we've picked up two significant customers in the past eighteen months. Without them we'd have been sunk. Also, you know we've had to take some drastic steps on our production side recently. One third of our factory staff has had to go.

'I don't want to have to go through the traumas of the past couple of years again. What I really need is some advice on how to tackle the future, how to become more efficient, tougher. Perhaps if I show you around the place and give you some facts and thoughts on Medway Menswear Ltd it will be a useful starting point for you. Let's start at the central office. While we're on the way I'll give you the basic information on our organisation, products and customers.

'The business was formed back in the 1920s by my grandfather who started manufacturing industrial clothing from very small premises on this site. From very small beginnings we're now proud of the fact that we are one of the biggest private companies in this industry. For some years now our turnover has been around the £8 million mark – although the sources of that turnover have changed somewhat.

'Our product lines now comprise suits, jackets and blazers, trousers and coats, overcoats and industrial uniforms. We supply "off the peg", made to measure, or via bulk orders, to a variety of customers including

High Street multiples and independents, mail order organisations and –
on the industrial side – health authorities and police departments. In a
way, I suppose, our varied customer and product base has been both
"saint and sinner" for us. Certainly we've watched many of our long-
established more narrowly-based friends in this industry go into liquidation over the past decade. We have, at least, managed to keep going.
However, being so varied gives us all sorts of production scheduling problems and generally seems to have left us – so far as production costs are
concerned – as a "jack of all trades and master of none".

'The mail order business, for example – trousers and jackets for the
catalogues – is probably no longer profitable. The retailers set the prices
to which we have to manufacture. They're the bosses in this industry. So
far as mail order is concerned, I think our cost structure is now too high
for us to manufacture profitably. Having said that, however, I have to
admit that we aren't totally sure about the profitability and contribution
of our various lines. Year end accounts have made it clear that some of
our pricing and costing has been "out of line".

'Of course, profits have only been part of our recent story. During the
really lean times, these orders undoubtedly help maintain capacity and
reduce overhead deficits. The business seems to become more and more
price competitive. I reckon that our prices, in real terms, haven't
increased in the past four years. It's so different to the days of 15 years
ago when people were taking all we could make. Of course, we can look
back now over the past 15 years and realise the massive effect changing
fashion has had on our business. Did you know, for example, that sales
of men's suits in the UK dropped from 10 million in 1970 to 4 million by
1980. During that period, of course, we were coming to terms with the
increasing threat of foreign imports – always substantially cheaper than
our offer and in the case of the East Europeans, often of pretty good
quality too. . . . This is the central office. They look after the accounts,
personnel records and customer orders in here. As you can see, a lot of
our office functions have been computerised recently – some government
grants were much appreciated. Computerisation has helped tremendously
with credit control and cash flow – a major problem for us. Thirty years
ago I seem to remember we never even required bank overdraft facilities.
During the past few years we've tended to strain our overdraft limits
persistently and we've used leasing facilities for our vehicles to help ease
the liquidity situation. We guess that we could improve this position if
we went public. Further share issues would also improve our gearing
position. However, we're proud of our "private" success and the directors
and management want the organisation to maintain its present control
structure . . .

'. . . Despatch, of course, handles the loading of the finished garments
into our vans for distribution. These days it's much more a case of filling
one van for one destination and one customer. The days when the van
visits a number of independent High Street retailers with a load of

smallish orders have dwindled. It's a reflection of our changing customer base which in turn is a reflection of what's happening on the High Street.

'The Department also receives raw materials – our basic cloths. They're waiting for a delivery now – cloth which is holding up production. It should have arrived a week ago. Suppliers are another difficulty. There aren't too many British cloth manufacturers left and the ones that are still producing aren't always as responsive to our needs as we'd like. I suppose if we were bigger, or if we could shop around a bit more the 'bargaining' relationship might change . . .

'The stock room these days is largely a sorting and clearinghouse sitting between the factory and despatch. Custômers used to visit us personally, select garments from the rails and take them away there and then. Again, this has changed. What you see on the rails here are mostly highly standardised garments waiting for the necessary requisition from our large retailer/mail order customers. Not so many years ago 40% of this stock would have been made to measure orders – thousands of customised "personally tailored" suits and jackets. This type of business now represents only 3% to 4% of our turnover – but we'd like to build this up a little because, provided we can meet the quality requirements in the "make" and avoid getting into a series of returns for alteration, this type of business makes us three times the profit earned from our standard "mass products".

'The top sector of the stock room is reserved for Bilton's garments. We're quite excited about our new venture with Bilton. It's a new departure for us – getting into retailing after more than a half century as a menswear manufacturer but, as you know, we now hold a "shop within shops" franchise in 27 of Bilton's South of England stores. Even though they take a hefty chunk of the retail "mark up" it still leaves us with a bigger margin than we're used to getting as simple manufacturers. Of course, what we have to do to take advantage of this opportunity is to sell as many of our garments as we can – and to produce and distribute them efficiently. Things look promising at the moment – in fact I think this venture has played a big role in our survival. However, we are still very much "learners" at this retail game. For example, we are targeting our garments at the 18–40 year old man, but to be honest, we aren't really sure what he's wearing, suit, jacket or trouser-wise, these days. Certainly our traditional view of quality with great attention to the make – things like an extra yoke or double lining – seems to be outdated. We take suggestions from Bilton's themselves about design and slowly we're learning what sells.

'Presently our franchise outlets are staffed by Bilton's people although we can, if we wish, introduce our own people. I do worry about the motivation of *their* staff towards selling *our* products and I think communications over things such as market and customer requirements could be improved.

'For almost 30 years now we have sold a range of our garments under the brand name of "tailor made". These brand garments have always been promoted as good quality, slightly up-market products and I think that, generally speaking, we have the production capability to do justice to this image. "Tailor made" garments are at the heart of our Bilton franchise. However, I'm a bit worried about the brand name itself. Isn't "tailor made" a little old-fashioned? Also one of our sales representatives was telling me last month how a customer had remarked that he had initially thought the brand name to have a Taiwanese "ring" to it.

'We undoubtedly also have many operational improvements to make within our Bilton's operation. One aspect that I should appreciate early advice on is that of stock control. You can see, for example, that we are holding thousands of pairs of trousers in the Bilton section of the stock department – I guess there must be around 16,000 garments hanging there now. I'm sure we could save money in the stockholding area – without, of course, jeopardising our overall sales position or, indeed, our relationship with Bilton.

'I'd better explain at this point, however, that the Bilton production set-up is a bit special. You know that we have recently cut back on our production capability (see Appendix 1.1). One way we've been able to do this and still maintain turnover is to contract out some of our work. In fact all the trouser production for the Bilton franchise is handled for us by Robert Hunt & Co Ltd – they're an old-established specialist trouser manufacturer based in Lancashire.

'I have some figures here which you might like to play around with, please. Let's see:

★ We sold 81,000 pairs of trousers through the Bilton's shops last year – at a fairly constant rate

★ Robert Hunt charges £5 per trouser

★ We estimate that our holding costs are about £10 per every 100 pairs of trousers

★ Re-ordering costs work out at about £50 each time. Although orders above 9,000 pairs (the maximum van capacity) incur additional charges of £40 per additional van journey

★ We wait on average, 20–30 days from order to delivery.

'Robert Hunt wrote to me last week saying they were prepared to offer us a 2% discount if we would agree to standardise the relationship into six deliveries per year . . .

'. . . We can have an uncluttered view of the production machinery here, at this time. It is, in the main, fairly old. We've computerised the office as you have seen, but the cost of making wholesale technological change in the production department, compared to the benefits and the payback period involved, is too high. We make improvements bit by bit as we can.

'Compared to competition which is able, and willing, to build factories in cheap labour countries, write off investment in tax relief and then move on when the country becomes less amenable, we are obviously at some disadvantage. While this is a problem area, I have to say that in my opinion this industry will remain labour intensive for some years to come.

'We also have an investment choice "on the boil". Jacket sewing, cutting and pressing equipment needs renewing and we're wondering which way to go. Using the present machinery and systems we reckon that our jacket line produces net profit of 6% pa. Jacket production is expected to hold steady at its present level of 100,000 garments per annum, for a number of years to come. Average jacket price is £15.

'We can replace, from Honers Ltd with identical equipment which will cost £250,000. A newer machinery supplier – Iztal (UK) Ltd – has also offered us a deal and will supply their equipment at a cost of £300,000.

'We believe that Iztal equipment will cut labour and energy costs and we'd expect these savings to increase our net profit margin by 1% to 7%.

'Both suppliers guarantee a six year life for their products. Of course, you know that cash flow is tight. We'd have to borrow from the bank to finance the investment. The bank will want its "pound of flesh" – 16% per annum at the moment.

'With which firm should we place the contract for the replacement machinery?

'I suppose this is where the 'bread is earned' – in the factory. We have 120 girls here usually, average age of about 19 years. Few seem to stay long after they get married. The maternity provision of a few years ago – The Employment Act, wasn't it? – worried us at the time – we've so many girls of the "right" age – but in the event I think we've come to terms with its effects.

'Absenteeism is running at 10%, which means we must maintain a reserve pool of machinists and our own small training school. Our girls come to be trained on leaving school at 16 – the usual pattern is for them to stay until they start their families, but very few return afterwards. We have been wondering about a job-sharing scheme to attract back mature skilled workers – there is a lot of loyalty to the firm in this area. Probably this would reduce absenteeism, but would the savings be swallowed up by extra personnel administration?

'We have briefly considered the issues of multi-skilling and/or group working but decided to stay with job specialisation. Fortunately, we've arrived at tea break time. It's much noisier when everything and everybody is working – and work they must. Productivity is essential. The girls start at 8.30 am and finish at 4.30 pm. In between they have one morning tea break of 15 minutes and a lunch break of 40 minutes. Other

Appendix 1.1(a) Medway Case Study
Present Value Factors – Interest Rates (1% to 14%)

Years	1%	2%	3%	4%	5%	6%	7%	8%	9%	10%	11%	12%	13%	14%
1	.9901	.9804	.9707	.9615	.9524	.9434	.9346	.9259	.9174	.9091	.9009	.8929	.8850	.8772
2	.9803	.9612	.9426	.9246	.9070	.8900	.8734	.8573	.8417	.8264	.8116	.7972	.7831	.7695
3	.9706	.9423	.9151	.8890	.8638	.8396	.8163	.7938	.7722	.7513	.7312	.7118	.6931	.6750
4	.9610	.9238	.8885	.8548	.8227	.7921	.7629	.7350	.7084	.6830	.6587	.6355	.6133	.5921
5	.9515	.9057	.8626	.8219	.7835	.7473	.7130	.6806	.6499	.6209	.5935	.5674	.5428	.5194
6	.9420	.8880	.8375	.7903	.7462	.7050	.6663	.6302	.5963	.5645	.5346	.5066	.4803	.4556
7	.9327	.8706	.8131	.7599	.7107	.6651	.6227	.5835	.5470	.5132	.4817	.4523	.4251	.3996
8	.9235	.8535	.7894	.7307	.6768	.6274	.5820	.5403	.5019	.4665	.4339	.4039	.3762	.3506
9	.9143	.8368	.7664	.7026	.6446	.5919	.5439	.5002	.4604	.4241	.3909	.3606	.3329	.3075
10	.9053	.8203	.7441	.6756	.6139	.5584	.5083	.4632	.4224	.3855	.3522	.3220	.2946	.2679
11	.8963	.8043	.7224	.6496	.5847	.5268	.4751	.4289	.3875	.3505	.3173	.2875	.2607	.2366
12	.8874	.7885	.7014	.6246	.5568	.4970	.4440	.3971	.3555	.3186	.2855	.2567	.2307	.2076
13	.8787	.7730	.6810	.6006	.5303	.4688	.4150	.3677	.3262	.2897	.2575	.2292	.2042	.1821
14	.8700	.7579	.6611	.5775	.5051	.4423	.3878	.3405	.2992	.2633	.2320	.2046	.1807	.1597
15	.8613	.7430	.6419	.5553	.4810	.4173	.3624	.3152	.2745	.2394	.2090	.1827	.1599	.1401
16	.8528	.7284	.6232	.5339	.4581	.3936	.3387	.2919	.2519	.2176	.1883	.1631	.1415	.1229
17	.8444	.7142	.6050	.5134	.4363	.3714	.3166	.2703	.2311	.1978	.1696	.1456	.1252	.1078
18	.8360	.7002	.5874	.4936	.4155	.3503	.2959	.2502	.2120	.1799	.1528	.1300	.1108	.0946
19	.8277	.6864	.5703	.4746	.3957	.3305	.2765	.2317	.1945	.1635	.1377	.1161	.0981	.0829
20	.8195	.6730	.5537	.4564	.3769	.3118	.2584	.2145	.1784	.1486	.1240	.1037	.0868	.0728

Appendix 1.1(b)
Present Value Factors – Interest Rates (15% to 50%)

Years	15%	16%	17%	18%	19%	20%	25%	30%	35%	40%	45%	50%
1	.8696	.8621	.8547	.8475	.8403	.8333	.8000	.7692	.7407	.7143	.6897	.6667
2	.7561	.7432	.7305	.7182	.7062	.6944	.6400	.5917	.5487	.5102	.4756	.4444
3	.6575	.6407	.6244	.6086	.5934	.5787	.5120	.4552	.4064	.3644	.3280	.2963
4	.5718	.5523	.5337	.5158	.4987	.4823	.4096	.3501	.3011	.2603	.2262	.1975
5	.4972	.4761	.4561	.4371	.4190	.4019	.3277	.2693	.2230	.1859	.1560	.1317
6	.4323	.4104	.3898	.3704	.3521	.3349	.2621	.2072	.1652	.1328	.1076	.0878
7	.3759	.3538	.3332	.3139	.2959	.2791	.2097	.1594	.1224	.0949	.0742	.0585
8	.3269	.3050	.2848	.2660	.2487	.2326	.1678	.1226	.0906	.0678	.0512	.0390
9	.2843	.2630	.2434	.2255	.2090	.1938	.1342	.0943	.0671	.0484	.0353	.0260
10	.2472	.2267	.2080	.1911	.1756	.1615	.1074	.0725	.0497	.0346	.0243	.0173
11	.2149	.1954	.1778	.1619	.1476	.1346	.0859	.0558	.0368	.0247	.0168	.0116
12	.1869	.1685	.1520	.1372	.1240	.1122	.0687	.0429	.0273	.0176	.0116	.0077
13	.1625	.1452	.1299	.1163	.1042	.0935	.0550	.0330	.0202	.0126	.0080	.0051
14	.1413	.1252	.1110	.0985	.0876	.0779	.0440	.0254	.0150	.0090	.0055	.0034
15	.1229	.1079	.0949	.0835	.0736	.0649	.0352	.0195	.0111	.0064	.0038	.0023
16	.1069	.0930	.0811	.0708	.0618	.0541	.0281	.0150	.0082	.0046	.0026	.0015
17	.0929	.0802	.0693	.0600	.0520	.0451	.0225	.0116	.0061	.0033	.0018	.0010
18	.0808	.0691	.0592	.0508	.0437	.0376	.0180	.0089	.0045	.0023	.0012	.0007
19	.0703	.0596	.0506	.0431	.0367	.0313	.0144	.0068	.0033	.0017	.0009	.0005
20	.0611	.0514	.0433	.0365	.0308	.0261	.0115	.0053	.0025	.0012	.0006	.0003

than for these "rest periods" it's "heads down". Every making and trimming operation has been "work studied" so that no girl has an operation which lasts more than two minutes. An important part of the process arrives at the end when each girl drops a card into her basket and so records further points towards her piece rate bonus. It's hard work but I hope, and think, that they are a very happy bunch. I like to think "Medway" is a family to *all* who work here and a close friend of the local community.

'Certainly, we have few union problems and, as managing director of an organisation which has pulled itself through some very difficult times, largely because its people have accepted changes and pulled together, I feel a strong obligation towards protecting the future of Medway Menswear Ltd and its people . . .'

2 · Sellafield and social responsibility

Bill Richardson and Tony Fowler

The issue of whether or not it is acceptable to expand or even to retain nuclear power as a source of energy provision is now a contentious issue in many countries. Whilst the strength of feeling on this issue does vary from country to country the battle between interested pressure groups can be seen throughout Europe. A major lesson that can be drawn from the 1980s experience in Chernobyl is that this is an international problem that cannot be contained by national frontiers.

The main question to be asked is whether the power generation company and/or country concerned should feel free to choose the mix of power provision it wishes or whether it should be constrained by wider social considerations. Whether the decision-makers are pursuing a least cost strategy, or one based upon other criteria either simple or complex, should they also be required to act in a socially responsible manner? If the answer to this question is 'yes', the wider question of what constitutes an acceptable level of social responsibility must then be addressed.

Before exploring this issue in somewhat more detail with the use of a specific example, certain factors should be borne in mind.

1 When nuclear power was first utilised for electricity generation, only a few decades ago, it was considered to be a very expensive alternative to other fuels and was only persisted with in order to gain experience and facilitate the further development of the new technology.

2 At that time, comparatively little was known about the dangers of nuclear power generation or the consequences of even minor accidents for the workforce or the surrounding population.

3 Investment in a power station is a very long-term decision whereas relative fuel prices can change dramatically over a comparatively short period (eg the effect of OPEC upon the choice between oil and coal). This means that it might be unwise to install only one type of fuel system even if it is least cost at the time of the investment.

4 The producers of fuels, be they domestic producers or foreign suppliers, can possess considerable bargaining power. This may be another argument for a diversified power base.

5   Decisions concerning the installation of power stations must be based upon long-term forecasts of the demand for energy which in turn depend upon long-term forecasts of the level of economic activity and trends in the mix and efficiency of energy utilisation. Such forecasts are highly speculative.

We will now explore the issues more thoroughly by examining the problems encountered in 1986 concerning the Sellafield Nuclear Power Station.

Sellafield and nuclear power

The Government-owned British Nuclear Fuels Ltd Sellafield (formerly Windscale) Plant is one of the world's oldest nuclear power stations. The technology at Sellafield is rather old and the station has had a controversial history, during the course of which there have been a number of 'scares' arising from accidental radioactive leaks. During the early part of 1986 another series of leaks produced a crisis for the organisation and the Government. In one incident a worker received the equivalent of a year's normal dose of radioactivity when he inhaled a quantity of plutonium gas which had escaped in a building on the site. In another incident 250 gallons of contaminated water had gushed from a broken pipe and created, according to the plant's operators '. . . an increase in radioactivity in the immediate vicinity'.

News of the accidents produced a variety of reactions from different interest groups.

(a) Environmental pressure groups

A spokesman for Greenpeace, the international conservation group, called for Sellafield to be shut down '. . . so that investigations can be carried out by the Nuclear Installations Inspectorate and the Radio-Chemical Inspectorate into the state of the plant and machinery involved in the Sellafield complex'. The spokesman continued '. . . Greenpeace believes that we can no longer depend upon the management of British Nuclear Fuels to safeguard the public from the radioactive hazards posed by the plant and therefore calls for the immediate removal of the senior management team . . . the BNFL Public Relations Department has shown in the past that it has misled and deceived the public about the true nature of the accidents, and the Government must step in'.

Friends of the Earth, the British-based environmental group, argued that BNFL had shown itself to be incapable of running the plant without exposing workers and the public to unacceptable levels of risk.

The concern expressed by these organisations over the dangers of nuclear power had been echoed in other parts of Europe by similar pressure groups. In particular the success of the Greens Ecology Party in the Federal Republic of Germany has been partly based upon the seriousness with which the younger generation views the dangers of radioactive pollution. At present two political parties in the FRG, the Greens and the official opposition, the SPD, are pledged to end the German nuclear power programme. A recent opinion poll undertaken by the German Atomic Forum has indicated that 34% of the population wants to close the country's atomic plants. Since the accident at Chernobyl West Germans have manifested their nuclear distrust in ways ranging from protests over bequerel levels in sandpits to the fighting of pitched battles with riot police at nuclear sites. The international nature of this concern has also been reflected by both German and Dutch groups protesting at new nuclear projects in neighbouring France. The lack of significant concern in France, where, because of the absence of alternatives, there is a large nuclear power programme, is an interesting phenomenon. Perhaps it says something about the French character or the way in which the programme has been marketed?

(b) Political parties

The accidents at Sellafield produced protests from political parties from at home and overseas.

The then leader of the Irish Opposition, Mr Charles Haughey, urged the Irish Prime Minister, Dr Garret Fitzgerald, to demand the closure of Sellafield during a meeting that was already scheduled to take place between Dr Fitzgerald and Mrs Thatcher. Dublin's Lord Mayor, Mr Jim Tunney, announced plans for a meeting of all Irish local authorities along the country's east coast to discuss the growing concern about possible dangers from Sellafield. Mr Paddy Lalor, an Irish MEP, raised the Sellafield issue in the European Parliament in Strasbourg and obtained a vote in favour of its closure. Pressure grew in the Isle of Man for a substantial compensation claim to be made against the British Government in respect of damage to the environment and the tourist industry of the island as a result of events at Sellafield.

These protests are also echoed on a European scale both in terms of the German and Dutch cases listed above and the wider concern expressed by many countries at the time of the Chernobyl incident.

Within the UK, the opposition parties both expressed their concern. The Labour Shadow Environment Secretary, Mr Jack Cunningham, whose constituency contained Sellafield criticised plant management and demanded a more independent element for the overseeing of the nuclear industry. He felt that the application of the Official Secrets Act had bedevilled the nuclear industry and called for its use to be dropped. The Social Democrat/Liberal Alliance suggested that the plant should remain open but called for an impartial public inquiry into the incidents which had '. . . chipped away at public confidence'.

(c) The Sellafield workers and the Trade Union Movement

The workers at Sellafield had to weigh the safety of their members against the employment losses that would result from closure. Within the organisation the workers staged a one-day protest strike and one worker interviewed leaving the plant commented '. . . sure I'd work somewhere else – but can you tell me where?'. The general union position within the plant was to push for stricter safety conditions without risking the threat of closure. It must be remembered that Sellafield is in a high unemployment area and few people in the community wish to risk the destruction of the major employer beside which the longer-term threats posed by radiation leakages seem less tangible.

The trade union movement as a whole is able to take a more detached view since the closure of nuclear power stations would destroy some jobs but create others, for example in coal-mining. They would not, however, wish to make statements that could be interpreted as undermining the position of the Sellafield workers.

(d) The Government and the BNFL Management

The Government attempted to 'ride out the Sellafield storm'. The then Environment Secretary, Mr Kenneth Baker, interviewed on the BBC's *This Week, Next Week* programme, described the incident as 'minor' and denied any sort of secrecy '. . . I think they are very open'. He also made the point that '. . . the reprocessing has to go on. You just simply could not close it' and that '. . . I think that if the people of Sellafield were asked they might vote to close the European Parliament'. Mr Baker likened the fears of radiation to the fears of witchcraft in the Middle Ages.

Both the Government and the Sellafield Management emphasised the 'minor' nature of the incidents, the national need for a civil nuclear power industry and the great concern and practical steps taken to ensure safety. Mr Baker argued that this was the most regulated industry in the country.

The position of the *Sellafield Management* is reasonably clear. Like the workforce they do not wish to lose their jobs and do not believe that their safety standards are inadequate. The position of the CEGB which is responsible for commissioning and maintaining power stations is more complex. The CEGB is a public sector body that is not subject to all of the normal pressures of a competitive market-place. It must, of course, meet the normal Government guidelines for investment appraisal and in this industry in particular must make decisions that are consistent with Government policy in this area. No doubt the CEGB wishes to keep its costs down, diversify its energy supplies, and plan for a secure future. It is an interesting question to consider, however, whether if the CEGB were a private organisation free from Government constraints, it would still be opting for an expansion in its nuclear capacity. This is particularly true in the current economic environment which is characterised by the following:

- low economic growth rates;
- an increasing emphasis upon energy saving technology;
- the existence on the world market of very cheap coal supplies (especially from South Africa);
- the availability of cheap electricity imports from countries like France.

The position of the *Government* can best be understood by considering a number of the points made at the beginning of this case.

The Government must attempt to maintain the stock of power-generating facilities at an adequate level over the decades ahead. It must base its decisions upon uncertain forecasts of energy needs and fuel costs. With these considerations in mind it has chosen to attempt to maintain a balance between the types of power stations provided rather than opt for a simple least cost solution, which may indeed in the future turn out to be incorrect. Particular threats that the Government's current chosen strategy seeks to avoid are:

- external threats from foreign fuel suppliers, eg OPEC
- internal threats from powerful groups of workers, eg the coal miners.

The Government has clearly taken advice concerning the safety of nuclear power and has accepted the advice of those scientists who believe that the threat of a catastrophe is small. This is a similar position to that taken up by many governments in Europe (eg, France and Germany) but is one that is coming under increasing pressure. It has, for example, been damaged by evidence such as that presented by Dr Derek Jakeman, a physicist and former Sellafield employee. Dr Jakeman has furnished information showing that radioactive pollution in the 1950s was up to 40 times higher than had previously been estimated. Dr Jakeman also contends that in 1955 he and a colleague had taken Geiger counters home in order to measure radiation levels. Alarmed by the high readings, they had returned to work seeking further information but had been refused and threatened with dismissal!

Public concern at the threats from nuclear power has increased in recent years due partly to the increased knowledge now possessed by scientists concerning the effects of radiation. This can be seen from the unnecessary risks that were taken at nuclear tests in the 1950s and from earlier safety standards at power stations which have had to be revised upwards. Some people believe that our present state of knowledge is still incomplete and that in the future present safety standards may also prove to have been inadequate.

The Chernobyl disaster has clearly marked out nuclear safety as a central public issue.

3 · Everlasting Hardware plc

Maurice Brown and John Patterson

Everlasting Hardware plc is a recently acquired subsidiary of an American multi-national holding company. The company is functionally structured and located on a single site in south-west England, with a resident Managing Director. Most of the senior and middle management (including the MD) have long service records with Everlasting, going back long before the takeover. One major exception to this is the Marketing Manager, an American who was brought into the firm at the insistence of the holding company, just over a year ago. Since the take-over Everlasting has operated independently of the group, providing most services in-house.

The main links between subsidiary and group are via a Group-Audit Committee which annually reviews individual subsidiary performance and the Group Capital Budget Committee which vets all project proposals in excess of £250,000 and annual capital budget requests from subsidiaries in excess of £2m. Companies within the group are required to repatriate 60% of annual profit to the holding company and have discretionary disposal over the remaining 40% within the parameters indicated. Allocation of funds from the holding company is treated as commercial debt and subsidiaries are actively discouraged from gearing up beyond 50%. Experience to date has indicated that although group policy is to focus strongly on ROCE performance of subsidiaries the audit committee positively encourages product and market diversification/growth, and inter-subsidiary competition for funds.

Everlasting manufactures a long-established and well-known range of kitchen utensils which has a good reputation for quality and reliability. The range has not, however, been substantially changed over the past 10 years, and has increasingly been regarded as 'old-fashioned' by younger purchasers, who have tended to turn to imported products from France and Sweden. The firm has an established policy that not more than 50%, by value, of components will be bought in.

In an effort to improve its image, the firm is investing in the manufacture of a new high-quality range of saucepans, which will sell alongside its existing range, but at a higher price. For its existing range the manufacture of handles is contracted to an external supplier. However, for this new range the Managing Director feels that it would be a good opportunity to acquire in-house expertise. It is envisaged that the specifications of the new handles will improve on existing standards of heat resistance, texture, design and colours. The newly developed polymers used in injection-moulding the plastics have recently been patented and these patents could be purchased to prevent a competitor from developing a similar handle. The main problem for Everlasting is its lack of expertise in injection-moulding; eg, in processing high grade plastics temperature control is vital if degradation is to be avoided. The operation of the injection-moulding equipment is a highly skilled task and it takes six to nine months of training to produce operatives of an adequate standard. Twelve operatives will be needed to run the plant on two shifts. The nearest supply of trained labour is in the north-east of England, where similar plant is operated, but good workers are in short supply and command premium rates. It will also be necessary to recruit two technicians to supervise the day-to-day running of the plant, and here again good people are in very short supply. Such technicians normally have a degree in chemical engineering and are typically appointed at middle management level, reporting directly to the Production Manager.

The views of departmental heads have been thoroughly explored in the Product-Development and Approval Committee. The Managing Director, who is under pressure from the holding company to improve the image of Everlasting's products, is in favour of in-house manufacture, since he sees future uses of the process for other products. The Marketing Manager shares his view, seeing the new material as crucial for the firm's long-term product/market strategy. There is, however, strong opposition from the Production Manager and his staff, who favour buying in the new handles to avoid unnecessary disruption. The Personnel Manager also has severe reservations about the training and recruitment programme needed for in-house manufacture. Despite these conflicting views, appropriate financial and technical estimates have been produced, and these yield the following conclusions:

1   The product is thought to have a life-cycle of no more than ten years.

2   The polymer patents can be purchased for £120,000 (or licences obtained for £5,000 per year).

3   Unused space within the factory is available for the installation of new machinery. (This space has no alternative use.)

4   Tooling up and ancillary expenditure; ie, the purchase and installation of an injection-moulding machine, is estimated at £500,000.

5   Everlasting's traditional supplier could be used instead of in-house manufacture, in which case the purchasing officer is confident that he can negotiate a long-term contract price of about £20 per set of handles. (A 'set' of handles is defined by the number of pans in the range, eg if there are 15 pans in a set then a set of handles comprises 15 units.)

6 If the range remains in production for nine years or more initial costs will be entirely written off and machinery will have a zero scrap value, if eight years £2,500 and if six years, a scrap value of about £10,000.

7 Manufacturing costs per set of handles have been estimated as follows:

Years t1 to t3 inclusive; throughout this period there may be production run and quality control problems caused by lack of experience:

Unit costs build-up:

	Normal Prodn	Severe Problems	No Problems
Materials	£1.00	£1.75	£0.75
Direct labour	6.00	7.00	4.35
Fuel & power	0.50	0.75	0.40
Overhead[1]	2.50	2.50	2.50
Allocated general exps	0.90	0.90	0.90
Depreciation	7.00	7.00	7.00
	£17.90	£19.90	£15.90

Years t4 to t10 inclusive; during these periods there should be no problems and it can 'safely' be assumed that unit costs will be no more than £16 per set of handles.

The above calculations are based on an annual target of 11,000 sets of good handles per year (unit variable costs are constant in the range of 6,000–12,000 sets per year)

8 At the end of the product's life all staff hired should be retained within the company. There is, however, a small chance that some will be made redundant and that severance costs should be allowed for. If the project folds in t9 or t10 these would be £20,000, in t8 £15,000, or if it folds as early as t6 they could be much higher due to the difficulty of redeploying the numbers involved, say £60,000.

9 Under the current tax regime all initial outlays on patent purchase and tooling up can be written off on a 25% reducing balance basis over eight years. The corporation tax rate is 35%.

---

1 Overhead is broken down into the provision of training for direct labour from t1 to t3 and hiring of additional supervisors for the life of the product:

Training allocation	£0.50
Supervision	2.00
	£2.50

10   Sales of the final product are quite sensitive to the business cycle; in recession they could average as low as 4,000 sets per year (in this event short-time working would be introduced rather than lay-offs), whereas in boom times they could be as high as 14,000 sets per year (in this case, an extra shift would be required, or premium rate overtime), in normal conditions annual sales should be around 11,000 sets.

Other issues discussed by the appraisal committee revolved around problems likely to be faced if the patent is not purchased – the difficulty of working to tighter specification on a new component in which the company has no experience and the difficulties of quality control in the early stages of operation. The Marketing Manager considered the purchase of the patent to be crucial because he knew of several rival companies which were also considering up-grading their brands. If this happened it could be assumed that Everlasting's sales would be around 75% of the predicted levels. The senior Production Manager was quite confident that learning problems would be minimal and that production would be 'normal' after about six months, his line-foremen were not so sanguine and were arguing for considerably more conservative cost estimates. The Purchasing Manager responsible for capital items estimated a full year from order-installation-and-commissioning before the production of handles would be on stream. Hanging over the committee was the knowledge that the Managing Director was expecting a positive report to take up to the Group Capital Budget Committee.

To incorporate the numerous uncertainties the appraisal committee decided that some kind of sensitivity analysis was essential and a newly appointed young graduate in the marketing team suggested the expectational approach he had been schooled in at his polytechnic. He explained to the appraisal team that essentially this meant 'weighting' the possible outcomes by the 'likelihood' of their occurrence and estimating the weighted average value/outcome or as he called it the 'expected value'. He demonstrated that 'weightings' were based on management perceptions of the environment and persuaded the committee to co-operate. The results are listed below:

Production t1 to t3	Probability*	Unit Costs
Severe problems	0.5	£19.90
Normal production	0.4	17.90
No problems	0.1	15.90

*   Disputed by the Production Managers' (apart from the senior manager) more pessimistic view.

State of the Economy

	Probability	Annual Sales
Recession	0.25	4,000
Normal	0.5	9,000
Boom	0.25	12,000

Redundancy

	Probability
Redundancy	0.3
No redundancy	0.7

Project Life

	Probability
10 years	0.6
8 years	0.3
6 years	0.1

More pragmatic managers also insisted on a more traditional and 'easy to understand' approach, simply identifying key factors and measuring viability against different assumed values of these.

Appendix 3.1 *Group-Subsidiary Control Chart*

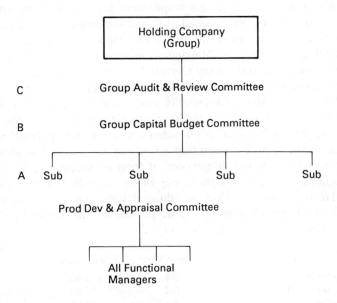

A   60% of all profit repatriated to group, discretionary use over rest subject to parameters in B

B   All projects >£250K must be submitted from subsidiaries for vetting. Annual capital budgets >£2M must be approved. The company imposed cost of capital on fund allocations is 20%. (The funding of the project would be entirely from Group and would be treated as a full-cost commercial loan. This should be treated as a 'hurdle' rate

as current commercial rates are substantially lower, eg between 12%
and 18% depending on the risk profile of the borrowing company.)
C   Reviews subsidiary performance. Main measure ROCE, but also
emphasise market and product growth/diversification

Appendix 3.2 *Industrial Relations At Everlasting*

The firm employs a total of 250 people on a single site. There has been
a long history of bad industrial relations at Everlasting, and the company
has experienced several major disputes. Prior to the takeover by an
American holding company three years ago, Everlasting had always
refused to formally recognise any trade union, and was notorious for low
wages and bad working conditions. As a result of this, labour turnover
was, and indeed remains, very high. Morale at shop floor level had never
been good, with most workers taking an anti-company stance and
complaining of 'high handed' and autocratic managements. After the
takeover Head Office in the States insisted on union recognition, in line
with their corporate policy, and the firm now pays minimum union rates
throughout the plant.

There have been two strikes since the takeover. The first of these was
a dispute about the 'clocking-in' system following a move by management
to deduct one hour's pay if any employee was late twice in the same
week. Production was stopped for three weeks before the matter was
resolved. The second strike was less protracted and began when an
engineer and two labourers were given instant dismissal because of
alleged abuse of a foreman. The men were reinstated on orders from the
Managing Director after four days.

The Managing Director is generally regarded as very reactionary, but
has had to modify his approach in recent years to avoid undue intervention from Head Office. He used the appointment of the new Marketing
Manager (who has replaced most of the marketing staff) as a warning of
further changes to come if he did not resolve some of the firm's long-term
problems. Other managers wish to continue with their 'traditional'
methods of working and urge him to take a harder line with Head Office,
who they believe would 'back-off' in the event of a showdown. Whilst
the Managing Director is sympathetic to their attitudes he also believes
that change will have to come and does not want to lose his job in the
process.

These disputes at senior management level have had unfortunate
effects on middle management who are generally dispirited and lack a
sense of direction. Marketing staff aside, most of them feel that union
recognition and the generally 'softer' line have made matters worse, in
that the discipline they are used to imposing is now openly resented and
resisted by the workforce.

4·Supergrip Tools Ltd

Peter L Jennings

This case was written from general experience by Peter L Jennings, Sheffield City Polytechnic. The case is intended for class discussion and not to illustrate either correct or incorrect handling of situations.

Situation in 1983

Following a management buy-out the new company, Supergrip Tools Ltd, commenced trading with an established product range, an established distribution system, established systems of manufacture and established, experienced, personnel. Quality had always been a key word in describing the product range and clearly the directors of Supergrip Tools wanted to maintain this view. However, due to the financial problems experienced up to 1983, it was thought necessary to clearly define the new firm to show that this was a new beginning and not merely an extension of Walker & Sons. Consequently, the name 'Supergrip Tools Ltd' was registered and the brandname changed to 'Supergrip'.

The product range could be divided into two broad categories:

(1) Heavy handtools – for example, vices, planes, G cramp and cramp heads

(2) Light handtools – for example, screwdrivers, chisels, gauges, bevels, decorator cutlery and so on.

Within each group there was a wide variety of individual items and wide variety of sizes available. For example, vices could be divided into four sub-divisions: mechanics, woodworking, pipe and hand vices; within each type up to ten different sizes or styles were available. Consequently there were over 1,750 different items offered for sale.

All heavy handtools were manufactured in one purpose-built relatively modern factory, constructed in 1980 in Dronfield on the southern outskirts of the city. The plant and equipment had been transferred to this new factory in 1980 from an older property which had been declared unsafe by the Building Inspectors. Thus, Supergrip Tools inherited a functional, single-storey, purpose-built factory unit, but machinery which dated back to the 1940s and 1950s. Many machines were out of date and inefficient by today's standards. However, skilled foremen and maintenance engineers kept the quality of output up to an acceptable level.

Approximately two-thirds of the light handtools were manufactured in another factory in the city centre. This building dated back to 1902 and had been in the hands of Walker & Sons up to 1983. Some of the original machinery was still in place although the power units had been changed from steam engine/belt drive to electric motors in the 1920s and 1930s. The factory was a three-storey building and a 'goods only' lift had been installed to facilitate movement of goods from floor to floor. This building tended to be cramped, dark and damp, but was functional. The company offices were also located on this site.

The remaining light handtools were purchased from other manufacturers and stored and distributed from the city centre site. Since it was intended initially to market the same product range, it was possible for Supergrip Tools to be sold via exactly the same distribution system as used by Walker & Sons. This consisted of six major categories of buyer:

(a) Buyers who required products to be branded with their own brandname

(b) Governmental departments, eg MOD

(c) Wholesalers

(d) Retailers

(e) Reciprocal traders – (who resold into the distribution system at another point without changing the product)

(f) Mail order and retail chains.

Each type of buyer stressed a different element in the marketing mix. For example, Government departments looked mainly for quality products to their specification, whilst wholesalers looked for low price. Thus the production facilities and selling team needed to be very flexible to cope with greatly differing demands. Physical distribution also required great flexibility to cope with demand for large and small batches of products and to cope with deliveries needing to be made from two separate factories.

The existing salesforce sold only in the UK and was organised on a geographical basis. Eight different regions had been identified in the UK mainland and one representative covered each region. Representatives were expected to sell all products to all potential buyers in their respective territories.

Financially, Supergrip Tools started life with a clean sheet. No sales or debts were carried over from Walker & Sons and the only money owing was £350,000 long term loan acquired from the 'Midwest' bank to buy the business. Additionally, £50,000 overdraft facility had also been negotiated to provide working capital if required in the early months.

During the last three years the workforce had been trimmed down considerably by natural wastage and redundancies (which, of course, contributed to the financial difficulties). This was partly a reflection of financial problems at Walker & Sons and partly a reflection of over-capacity in the factories. Indeed it was estimated that the factory produced only 50% of the available output during 1982. The total work-force inherited by Supergrip Tools was 75, including all managers, staff and workforce.

Developments up to June 1987

Initially, difficulties were experienced with suppliers of raw materials owed money by Walker & Sons. Although new directors were now running the company, some suppliers simply saw Supergrip Tools as Walker & Sons with a different name. Some refused to supply, whilst others demanded cash with order. A great deal of effort went into convincing suppliers that the new company was soundly based.

Similarly, many customers were reluctant to begin trading again, fearing that the new company would not survive for very long. The £50,000 overdraft facility was almost fully utilised in the first 6–9 months of trading. Fortunately, confidence gradually returned and sales over the first five years were as follows:

1983	1984	1985	1986	1987
£565,124 (10 months only)	£654,018	£785,448	£923,038	£1,041,023

Unfortunately, difficulties were also experienced with employees who could not accept the change in ownership and the determined approach of the new directors. Ingrained attitudes and philosophies proved difficult to change and initially hindered the development of Supergrip Tools. By early 1986, Julian Crabtree and his fellow directors had managed, through natural wastage and early retirement, to assemble a young enthusi-astic management team which made up for lack of experience by sheer determination. Fortunately, most of the skilled operators proved more flexible and with only one or two exceptions, all works personnel adapted and stayed with the company.

There appeared to be no radical changes in the types of buyers who purchased handtools in the UK, although foreign competition became stronger. Estimates of the total size of the UK market were as follows:

	1983 £'000	1984 £'000	1985 £'000	1986 £'000	1987 £'000
Basic Production	163,900	188,100	200,700	215,600	227,800
Plus Imports	53,830	70,983	85 637	94 259	99,749
	217,730	259,083	286,337	309,859	327,549
Less Exports	91,055	101,422	92,657	103,138	108,005
Estimated Home Market	126,675	157,661	193,680	206,721	219,544

Foreign competitors, mostly from the Far East and Eastern Europe, could be found in all segments of the market producing generally good quality but cheaper tools.

Until now lack of finance had made developments very limited and no major changes to factories, product ranges or the size of the workforce had been possible. However, good working relations had been established with a 'central core' of approximately 250 customers. In total approximately 1,500 accounts received some goods during the year. The reputation of Walker & Sons had been laid to rest and Supergrip now enjoyed normal commercial credit terms with all their suppliers.

At the management meeting, Diane Wilson, the Financial Director, was able to circulate the accounts for 1987 (Appendix 1). All of the bank overdraft facility had been repaid although only a very small amount of cash in hand existed at the bank. Diane had told the meeting that the 'Midwest' Bank was very pleased with their progress and were willing to consider an application for further loans for investment in the business. The question remained, however, in which directions could the company expand and what would be the likely consequences of expansion?

Appendix 4.1 *Manufacturing and Trading Accounts of Supergrip Tools for the Year Ending 31 December 1987*

	£	£	£
Sales			1,041,023
Stocks of raw materials at 1 Jan 87	10,143		
Purchases of raw materials	132,621		
	142,764		
Stocks of raw materials at 31 Jan 87	11,652		
		131,112	
Factory wages		312,570	
Depreciation of plant & equipt		20,000	
Factory Expenses		121,425	
		585,107	
Less Increase on work-in-progress		1,283	
		583,824	
Plus Stock of finished goods 1 Jan 87		45,186	
		629,010	
Less Stock of finished goods 31 Dec 87		47,987	
Cost of goods sold			581,023
Gross profit			460,000

Profit and Loss Account
for the Year Ending 31 December 1987

Gross profit		460,000
Admin exps		
(inc loan interest)	223,452	
Selling & distribution exps	116,548	
		340,000
Net profit c/d		120,000

Profit and Loss Appropriation Account
for the Year Ended 31 December 1987

Net profit for year		120,000
Less Corporation tax		55,000
Net profit for year after tax		65,000
Add Balance brought forward		5,000
Profits available for appropriation		70,000
Less Appropriations:		
Transfer to general reserves	30,000	
Proposed ordinary dividend	4,000	
		34,000
Balance carried forward to next year		36,000

Balance Sheet as at 31 December 1987

Share Capital			*Fixed Assets*		
Authorised &			Buildings		
issued		40,000	Cost	173,618	
			Depreciation	100,000	
Revenue Reserves					73,618
General	35,000				
Profit & loss			Plant & equip		
Appropriation	36,000	71,000	Cost	160,000	
			Depreciation	100,000	
					60,000
Long-term Loans[1]		150,000			
Current Liabilities			*Current Assets*		
Creditors &			*Stock*		
accrued exps	24,500		Raw materials	11,652	
Corp tax	55,000		Finished goods	47,987	
Prop dividend	4,000		Work-in-progress	6,791	
		83,500			66,430
			Debtors &		
			prepayments	143,211	
			Cash	1,241	
					144,452
		£344,500			£344,500

(1)   A proportion of the long-term loan has been repaid each year to date

5 · Rutshire County Council – Consumer Protection Department

Bill Richardson

This case study has been written from general experience. It is intended to be used as the basis for class discussion rather than as a comment on the handling of a business situation.

In 1982 Fred Hartley looked back with some pride – and some regret – over his career.

As Chief Officer of Rutshire County Council's Consumer Protection Department since local government reorganisation in 1974, Fred had been responsible for the integration of the old Weights and Measures Departments of the four major towns in Rutshire (Malchester, Ronfield, Drayton and Cranthorpe) and the subsequent operation of the county-wide service.

Not surprisingly the county structure had been headed by 'weights and measures men' most of whom Fred knew as Malchester colleagues or members of the 'tightly knit' Institute of Trading Standards Administration. The identities of the former local town services had been maintained via the creation of town-based divisions organised on a functional basis and linked to a new, centrally situated, head office at Dortown. Appendix 5.1 gives details in the form of an organisation chart.

In the mould of its mother organisation (Rutshire County Council) the Department was based on clear hierarchies of seniority and communication links and voluminous rules and job descriptions. Such structural characteristics remained fundamental (and became a focal point in any disputes) although a less formal structure exhibiting much lateral communication and discretion as to which jobs to tackle and how to perform them had also evolved. Divisional staff worked closely together in the same premises and through the facility of 'car user allowance' were highly mobile across divisions. Quick meetings, discussions during chance meetings and telephone conversations were preferred to more formal lines and methods of communication. The nature of many of the working problems faced by field staff demanded initiative, speed and flexibility. Appendix 5.2 illustrates some of the areas of operation.

The first four years of the new Department had been almost idyllic. NALGO (National Association of Local Government Officers) was strong but not particularly militant. Job security was high – nobody ever 'got the sack' from Rutshire. Staff control, potentially difficult given the history and nature of many of the people employed and the jobs to be done, had never been a problem. The predominantly young people of the Department (average age in 1975 had been less than 30) had emerged from their Weights and Measures localised environments into a wider and better resourced consumer protection operation. Most received some form of promotion and/or salary increase and many (particularly those who were redeployed in the Consumer Affairs Section) found the newer areas of consumerism (eg, Trade Descriptions, Consumer Credit, Consumer Advice, Research and Publicity) stimulating. New staff recruited from business and higher education for the skills and experience they could bring to these newer functions were also keen to do a good job and happy to be in 'the sort of occupation which gives you a worthwhile job and lets you get on with doing it'.

The later years of Fred's 'reign', however, were characterised by growing 'rumblings' of disquiet.

While 1974's reorganisation had produced a very attractive package of benefits for everyone, nothing much had improved since then. The Department was generally recognised as being the poor relation in comparison to major county functions such as Highways and Environment and with central sources of funds becoming increasingly scant the early euphoria of growth and development was soon curtailed. Appendix 5.5 gives some comparative budgetary and manpower information.

Morale of staff was also affected by increasing workloads. As advice/complaint enquiries rose from levels of 22,000 per year to 40,000 per year, staff involved in these work areas began to resent 'having too much of the same thing to do'. New pieces of consumer legislation introduced in the 1970s and early 1980s – without any accompanying additional resources – added to the Department's already extensive catalogue of legislative obligations and duties. Staff complained about the lack of policy direction on the issue of which of the competing work objectives of quality and quantity should be given priority. They remained suspicious, too, about the computerised record-keeping system which emphasised, in statistical form, the volume of work performed.

Further, Fred had noted a growing resentment from the non Weights and Measures sections of his staff about the traditional practice which precluded anyone other than a Weights and Measures qualified person from obtaining a managerial position in the organisation. Appendix 5.3 gives some information on the types of people employed in different sections of the Department.

Non-'ticket'-holders, particularly from the Consumer Affairs section, were voicing their resentment of their perceived 'second class' status. Certainly job turnover was highest in this section although this was variously ascribed to a number of factors including:

– the training, nature and qualifications of these personnel made the securing of outside occupations more natural and easy

- motherhood (a significant proportion of the section was female)
- the desire to leave what might otherwise be a long-term career because of the lack of advancement opportunities.

Managers involved in selection procedures maintained that the promotion/advancement situation had been covered in selection interviews although this assertion was disputed by some 'non-qualified' staff members.

Generally, staff morale was reducing.

Matters became particularly tense over issues of accountability when staff objected to a directive insisting on better record-keeping. Accusations of a broken promise that the recent introduction of computerised record-keeping would not lead to computer statistics being used for individual appraisal and control purposes were levied at Fred personally. A dispute over job descriptions and short manning led to his handing in his NALGO 'hat' to concentrate more clearly on his managerial function. In 1982, with some misgivings, the 'wise old owl' of Rutshire's Consumer Protection Department took early retirement.

The new regime

Charles Crawley was in his early 40s, ambitious, bright and hard working. His professional career had been spent in local authority trading standards enforcement work. Weights and Measures qualified and a member of the Institute of Trading Standards Administration, Charles' appointment to the position of Chief Officer of Rutshire's Consumer Protection Department provided him with experience of a third local authority system. Some of the internal, defeated candidates were openly disparaging of his more aggressive approach and of his 'careerist' route to the top of Consumer Protection ('moving loyalties to get twice as far in half the time'). His ambition and dynamism, however, was seen as appropriate to the more positive presentation of the Department's public face during a period when the County Council itself was engaged in a campaign against the Government's plans to abolish the Metropolitan County Councils. Charles acknowledged the wealth of resources and reputation which had been developed by Rutshire's Consumer Protection Department over the years and looked forward to developing these aspects further. He immediately set about the task of creating 'his team'. Very astutely, according to some observers, he selected an 'inner circle' of about 10 people (all Weights and Measures men with the exception of the Home Economist). These people were drawn away from their traditional duties and spent increasing proportions of their time working from Head Office. Much emphasis was placed on showing a public face and on finding newsworthy situations to report. To many it now seemed that someone from the 'upper echelon' was always on local TV, radio or in the newspapers. Further forays by Charles to the extremes of his organisation brought in other officers for the purpose of developing 'projects'. These changes were made quickly and informally. Attempts to attain a useful and formally recognised new structure, however, were consistently resisted by union representatives and by the staff in free votes on proposed changes.

A new sense of vibrancy permeated the organisation. Its external face was one of proactivity, professionalism and concern for the consumer. Internally, the status of officers now depended upon their closeness to Charles and their associations with the increasingly important functions of publicity and projects. Traditional duties seemed to be taking a back seat.

Most of those 'pulled out' for projects by Charles welcomed their new status and job enrichment. Many left at the periphery of the organisation, however, began to feel resentful. Now even fewer officers were left at Divisional level to perform the ongoing, everyday, tasks. Fewer inspections were being carried out – those Inspectors left at Divisions refused to cover the areas left by their seconded colleagues. At the Advice Centres consumer advisers found themselves managing much of the time without their senior advisers in attendance. They also complained about the extra work being generated by the new levels of publicity and of often 'finding out what the Department had said to the media the day before' from the customers coming into the Advice Centres. They also pointed out the paradox of being left to manage under a system which refused to accept their pertinence as managers. As point of first contact for 95% of the Department's customers they felt angry about being left on the perimeter of the organisation 'to get on with it'.

For the first time in its history the Department's Advice Centres began closing for lunch. On a couple of occasions, because relief staff from other sections were either unavailable or unwilling to cover, the Ronfield Centre closed its doors during normal working hours. Previously, flexible cover of this nature had always been available as a matter of course. Many advisers began operating as pure advisers (rather than as assistors/interventionists). Two Divisionally-employed Weights and Measures Inspectors left Rutshire for similar posts with other authorities.

In 1984 a rare vacancy in the Consumer Affairs section produced a recruitment advertisement which again restricted the class of applicants to Weights and Measures qualified personnel. A memo expressing concern over the continuation of this 'restrictive practice' signed by 30 staff members drawn from Consumer Affairs, Enforcement and Clerical sections was handed to Charles and set in motion a series of meetings between Charles and the Departmental representatives over the issue. Subsequently, a new advertisement was published offering the post of Senior Trades Descriptions Officer at Ronfield Division to Weights and Measures qualified applicants *plus* other appropriately qualified/experienced personnel. The post, which had been 'blacked' was opened up and attracted a number of internal applicants. Appendix 5.4(i) provides brief CV details of the applicants (all of whom were interviewed).

John Treeton was offered the job and he accepted. Many of the other candidates referred to the selection process and the interview as 'a joke process'.

Generally John's new colleagues were disappointed to find that John spent much of his time on project work for Charles rather than on the traditional aspects of trade descriptions work. Within three months of the appointment, Lawrence Hinds had left the Department to work for a national finance company.

Shortly after the Ronfield position had been filled the similar post at Cranthorpe became available. Appendix 5.4(ii) gives details of candidates. James Fox was appointed.

Meanwhile, the vacancy created by John Treeton's appointment and transfer also formed the basis of a recruitment and selection procedure. This senior advisory officer post was strongly expected to provide *the* major breakthrough – the appointment of a non Weights and Measures person to a senior, managerial position. Culturally this post was furthest away from the traditional Weights and Measures bastions of inspection and law enforcement. It was also acknowledged as offering 'some of the hardest work to be had in the Department'. Candidates are considered briefly in Appendix 5.4(iii).

Russell Hardcastle was appointed to the post.

Within six months Ruth Jones had left to join a business education consultancy firm and William Bright had secured a position as a legal executive with another local authority.

Much time was spent (during working hours) discussing the situation of the non-qualified staff. William summed up the feelings of many of his colleagues. 'This is a good job, basically. We have a free hand, by and large, and you can really do a good job for the people and the community. The problem is, is that the job needs self-motivation and after a while of being treated 'second class' you feel it's stupid bothering. Why should we graft when others are assured of the recognition and rewards – particularly when you feel that you're better than them at the job and basically more committed to it?'.

A number of 'non-qualified' staff commenced a mass grievance procedure against Charles. Soon after, the Cranthorpe senior advisory post was advertised. Only three people applied for the job – all internal candidates and all 'non-qualified' Consumer Affairs staff.

Roy Dale (formerly the Consumer Credit Officer at Cranthorpe) duly became the first 'non-qualified' manager of the Rutshire Consumer Protection Department.

Within a year the entire Department was dismantled and rehoused in various forms in the original borough councils of the county. In accord with Government plans Rutshire County Council was abolished in 1986.

Appendix 5.1 *Rutshire County Council Consumer Protection Department Organisation Structure*

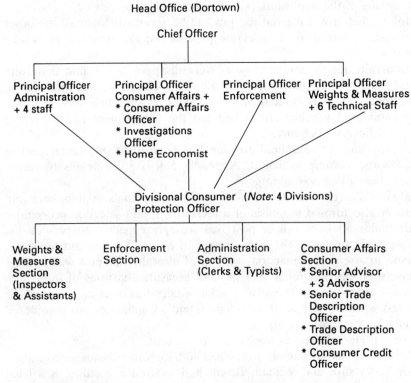

Head Office (Dortown)

Chief Officer

| Principal Officer Administration + 4 staff | Principal Officer Consumer Affairs + * Consumer Affairs Officer * Investigations Officer * Home Economist | Principal Officer Enforcement | Principal Officer Weights & Measures + 6 Technical Staff |

Divisional Consumer (*Note*: 4 Divisions) Protection Officer

| Weights & Measures Section (Inspectors & Assistants) | Enforcement Section | Administration Section (Clerks & Typists) | Consumer Affairs Section * Senior Advisor + 3 Advisors * Senior Trade Description Officer * Trade Description Officer * Consumer Credit Officer |

Appendix 5.2

PUSHCHAIR SURVEY
Findings Give Cause for Concern
Many parents could be pushing their children
around in faulty or even unsafe pushchairs.
They could also be misusing the pushchair
to the detriment of the child and the pushchair.

You may have heard or read recently that this department intended to carry out Pushchair MOTs and understandably wondered what it was all about. Well, it all began when we received a serious complaint about a pushchair which caused a child to loose the ends of two fingers. As a result of this and other complaints about pushchairs, we decided to carry out a modest survey to discover if these complaints were isolated incidents or if there really was cause for concern over the safety, standard and use of pushchairs.

The county-wide checks, which involved examining pushchairs in use and talking to parents, revealed that there is cause for concern. Of all the pushchairs examined (nearly all were the baby-buggy type) 81% were found to be faulty and 25% were declared unfit for use. To make matters worse the majority of these faults were found on pushchairs under 1 year old and yet most parents expected their pushchairs to last 2–3 years. Faults, however, were not the only problem; there were also many examples of misuse on the owner's part such as heavy shopping bags hanging from the handles causing instability and strain.

The information we have collected obviously points to a need to improve the standard of baby-buggy type pushchairs and so we will be making representations to manufacturers, the British Standard Institution and the Department of Trade. In the meantime, you can read the details of our findings, our comments and advice on pages 2 and 3 and if you are thinking of buying a pushchair, our special Pushchair Price Survey could save you money.

ONE DAY SALES

In the weeks before Christmas you may well find a leaflet pushed through your letter-box advertising a One Day Sale in a local pub or church hall. If the leaflet proclaims unbelievable bargains like continental quilts from £2.00, Black and Decker drills from £5.00, toasters from £1.00, be very wary. These bargains sound too good to be true and they usually are, as none of the advertised goods are ever offered for sale. 'The van broke down on the way here' is often one of the excuses given for the lack of these advertised goods.

This type of one day sale should not be confused with the well-established one day sales that are often held in hotels and well advertised in the local press. At this type of sale the goods are on display and clearly marked with their price and can be examined. At the type of sale we are warning you about, the goods are never on display but are placed on a table beside the salesman on the stage.

The salesman who will tell the audience several times it is a sale, not an auction, will get the attention of the crowd by offering for sale items at much less than they are worth. Unfortunately, having got the audience interested, the salesman will eventually be able to sell them goods that are worth far less than the amount paid. A radio sold for £15 but worth only £5 and a set of crockery also sold for £15 retailing at £4 in a local shop are just two examples of how these fast-talking, persuasive salesmen take people for a ride and make a huge profit for themselves.

So if you are tempted to attend one of these sales, do not get carried away by the sales patter, and ask yourself if you are really getting a bargain. You can probably buy the same goods more cheaply locally, and you will know where to find the seller if you have a complaint.

If you do get a leaflet pushed through your letter-box advertising a one day sale, would you let us know immediately, and then one of our officers can attend the sale to see if any offences are committed?

CHRISTMAS IS COMING
Once again we will be carrying out special Christmas Price Surveys to help you save time and money at Christmas.

The first Christmas Price Survey to be published will be on Toys and Games. Although we have carried out this survey for several years the savings to be made by shopping around never fail to amaze us ....

IN THIS ISSUE
The consumer information magazine which provides the news, advice and information, enabling you to buy wisely, looks at ....

Bills and Debts

It is so easy for bills to mount up, but what can you do if you are not able to pay them?

Glittering Lamps

Are they a hazard? See our findings.

Cars

Thinking of buying a car this summer? Read our article before you do.

Shoes

'My shoes are killing me' – a familiar cry – our 'Help Yourself' column and 'Mrs Price' provide some useful information on buying shoes.

Miles per Gallon

Did you know there are new regulations in force regarding information about the fuel consumption of cars?

Appendix 5.3 *Rutshire County Council Consumer Protection Department Staff Profile*

Weights and Measures Qualified Staff

Approximately 40 of the 120 staff employed by the department held the Weights and Measures 'ticket' – a qualification with statutory backing and awarded by the Department of Trade. Traditionally the 'ticket' had been associated with the Weights and Measures Act 1963 and the inspectorate duties contained therein. A recent ruling by the Inspectors' Association (Institute of Trading Standards Administration) had insisted that only graduates were eligible to train as Weights and Measures Inspectors (a minimum two years on-the-job/study/exam programme).

All managerial jobs (except those in Admin and Personnel) were allocated to Weights and Measures 'ticket-holders'. Managers' vacancies were advertised exclusively to those holding the qualification and so ensured a managerial route for those Weights and Measures people currently employed in the traditional role of 'Inspectors'. Weights and Measures Inspectors commanded one grade higher, on the salary scale premium than other 'field' professionals. Generally, 'ticket-holders' were a very tightly knit group of professionals who sought to maintain the status of their important but occupation-specific qualification.

Weights and Measures Assistants

Traditionally, each Weights and Measures Inspector had an assistant to take the burden of some of the more onerous duties involved in the Weights and Measures function (eg, carrying heavy weights, shovelling coal in coal weight checks, etc). This tradition had been maintained and the Department employed around 20 such staff – 'a silent army'.

Consumer Affairs Staff

Apart from the managerial posts in this section the staff employed came from a variety of backgrounds with a wide range of experience and qualifications (eg MSc, BA, HND, AIB (Associate Institute of Bankers), ACIS (Associate Chartered Institute of Secretaries), Teaching Certificate). They worked in the newer areas of consumerism from the county's prestigious Advice Centres performing duties associated with consumer advice, trade descriptions, consumer credit and research/publicity. Such staff were encouraged to study for the Diploma in Consumer Affairs. Rewards for the attainment of such a qualification were advancement to the next year's point on the salary scale and, for Consumer Affairs staff, removal of the bar which stopped staff moving up the Admin and Professional salary grades and, perhaps into the first tier of the Senior salary range.

Three 'non-qualified' Consumer Affairs staff were employed at Head Office.

Enforcement Officers

The county employed 12 enforcement officers whose jobs were associated with the enforcement of Consumer Safety and Food and Drugs legislation. Most of these employees were long-service people who had trained as Weights and Measures Inspectors in the days before the graduate entry ruling but who had not attained the 'ticket' qualification.

Clerical and Administration

Headed by a Principal Officer based at Head Office (holding the Diploma in Public Administration) this section provided back-up support to the 'field' officers.

Appendix 5.4 *Rutshire County Council Consumer Protection Department Vacant Post Candidates*

(i) *Post of Senior Trade Descriptions Officer, Ronfield*

Candidates	CV Details
George Hunt	46 years, 10 years experience at TDO (Trade Descriptions Officer) in Malchester office. No formal qualifications. Useful record in post.
Brian Rogers	41 years. Originally a W & M trainee with another local authority but did not obtain W & M 'ticket'. For past 10 years worked as TDO in Cranthorpe. Had run this section during past vacancies and had provided induction training for his two previous Senior TDO's. Excellent record in trade description work and well respected by other staff.
Lawrence Hinds	31 years. 8 years within the Ronfield TD section specialising in Consumer Credit but doing much TD work also. Useful record of TD investigations and prosecutions. Together with Gary Andrews (see below) had been running the section during the present vacancy of the past 6 months. AIB + teaching certificate.
William Bright	30 years. 8 years in Drayton office (4 as an adviser, last 4 as Consumer Credit Officer also working in TD matters). Successful general and TD-related record. BABS (Hons) and Diploma in Consumer Affairs.
Gary Andrews	27 years. TD Officer for previous 10 months in Ronfield. Previously Technical Officer at HO and prior to this sergeant in Army.
Andrew Marples	38 years, Weights and Measures Inspector at Cranthorpe office for past 9 years.
John Treeton	Weights and Measures qualified plus DCA. Presently Senior Consumer Adviser at Drayton and a successful record in this post over past 10 years. Of late had been spending an increasing amount of time on project work and central publicity. Had liaised with TD section at Drayton but little practical experience in the field and no track record.

(ii) *Senior Trade Descriptions Officer, Cranthorpe*

Andrew Marples	(as 4(i))
George Hunt	(as 4(i))
Brian Rogers	(as 4(i))
Gary Andrews	(as 4(i))
David Eccles	32 years, past 8 years as W & M Inspector at Drayton.
James Fox	Almost identical to John Treeton but Senior Advisory post at Cranthorpe.

(iii) *Senior Advisory Officer, Drayton*

Russell Hardcastle	33 years, W & M Inspector for past 6 years in Malchester office. Had spent approximately half a day per week over past 6 months helping out in the Malchester Advice Centre.
William Bright	See Details in Appendix 4(i)
George Anderson	30 years. Formerly an assistant in Drayton Advice Centre. Had been a mainstay in the continued operation of Drayton Advice Centre during recent months. DCA held.
Ruth Jones	28 years. Past two years as Consumer Adviser in Cranthorpe. BA.
Alan Fieldman	55 years. An Advisory Officer from the pre-1974 days when Malchester had formed the first consumer advice centre in the country. Well respected and used to managing the busy Malchester centre during the frequent illness-forced absences of the present Malchester Senior Adviser.

Appendix 5.5 *Rutshire County Council – Revenue Expenditure 1980/81 to 1984/85*

COMMITTEE Gross expenditure	1980/81 (£'000)	%	1981/82 (£'000)	%	1982/83 (£'000)	%	1983/84 (£'000)	%	1984/85 (£'000)	%
Consumer protection	1,540	1	1,686	1	1,920	1	1,979	1	2,079	1
Environment	6,137	4	5,596	3	6,758	3	6,535	3	7,198	3
Fire service	11,742	7	13,519	7	15,697	6	16,656	7	18,032	6
Highways	43,931	26	49,679	25	56,993	24	57,713	24	59,590	22
Passenger transport	49,033	29	61,780	31	73,825	31	77,265	32	73,595	27
Planning	1,547	1	2,438	1	2,733	1	2,844	1	2,834	1
Less Recharges	–	–	705Cr	–	799Cr	–	848Cr	–	810Cr	–
Police	43,142	25	50,014	26	57,680	24	63,369	26	94,054	34
Policy										
Central establishment	7,826	4	8,027	4	8,908	4	9,487	4	9,659	3
Less Recharges	7,568Cr	4Cr	7,814Cr	4Cr	8,637Cr	4Cr	9,144Cr	4Cr	9,274Cr	3Cr
Probation	3,865	2	4,489	2	5,084	2	5,507	2	6,005	2
Other services	5,542	3	6,516	3	7,400	3	7,604	3	7,856	3
Recreation, culture and health	1,251	1	1,303	1	1,640	1	2,112	1	2,677	1
	167,978	99	196,528	100	229,202	96	241,079	100	273,495	100
Contribution to capital fund	2,553	1	–	–	–	–	–	–	–	–
Contribution to renewal & repairs fund	–	–	–	–	10,000	4	–	–	–	–
Provision for bad debts	–	–	–	–	40	–	–	–	–	–
	170,531	100	196,528	100	239,242	100	241,079	100	273,495	100

Appendix 5.5 (continued)

Financed from										
*Precept	123,720	72	78,887	40	96,093	40	103,345	43	113,665	42
*Government grants	38,485	23	108,420	55	121,885	51	116,278	48	137,384	50
Other income	13,271	8	13,162	7	16,162	7	16,969	7	17,709	7
Contribution from renewal & repairs fund	–	–	–	–	–	–	900	–	3,093	1
Appropriation of DLO balances	–	–	–	–	–	–	–	–	900	–
Utilisation of miscellaneous receipts	–	–	–	–	–	–	–	–	744	–
	4,945Cr	3Cr	3,941Cr	2Cr	5,102	2	3,587	2	–	–
Balances	170,531	100	196,528	100	239,242	100	241,079	100	273,495	100

Appendix 5.6 *Rutshire County Council – Capital Expenditure 1980/81 to 1984/85*

COMMITTEE	1980/81 (£'000)	%	1981/82 (£'000)	%	1982/83 (£'000)	%	1983/84 (£'000)	%	1984/85 (£'000)	%
Gross expenditure										
Consumer protection	79	1	22	–	72	–	97	1	5	–
Environment	2,055	12	2,246	11	2,301	10	2,879	13	1,684	8
Fire service	95	1	199	1	1,540	6	1,359	6	1,813	9
Highways	8,948	51	11,394	58	11,837	50	11,688	52	13,011	65
Highways – Direct labour organisation	–	–	56	–	643	3	174	1	8	–
Passenger transport	–	–	–	–	200	1	–	–	128	1
Planning	–	–	–	–	–	–	–	–	–	–
Police	2,545	14	3,246	17	3,402	14	2,569	11	1,623	8
Policy										
Central establishment	192	1	478	2	783	3	108	1	107	1
Probation	25	–	21	–	13	–	25	–	164	1
Other services	3,399	19	1,878	10	1,688	7	1,660	7	1,019	5
Recreation, culture and health	89	1	239	1	1,317	6	1,824	8	522	2
	17,427	100	19,779	100	23,796	100	22,383	100	20,084	100
Financed from										
Loan	8,321	48	14,420	73	19,675	83	18,823	84	14,445	72
Government grants	3,252	19	2,273	11	1,303	5	2,987	13	4,645	23
Capital receipts	194	1	146	1	395	2	181	1	324	2
Capital fund	5,467	31	–	–	–	–	–	–	–	–
Revenue	435	2	2,826	14	2,416	10	259	1	69	1
Balances	242Cr	1Cr	114	1	7	–	133	1	601	3
	17,427	100	19,779	100	23,796	100	22,383	100	20,084	100

Appendix 5.7   *Rutshire County Council Budget Summary 1985/86*

	1985/86 Estimate (£'000)
NET REQUIREMENTS	
Transportation	
Highways	34,380
Less: Transport	
Supplementary grant	(3,838)
	30,542
Passenger transport	78,050
	108,592
Less: Transport	
Supplementary grant	—
	108,592
Other services	
Consumer protection	1,822
Environment	3,974
Fire service	16,079
Planning	1,737
Police	29,699
Policy	
Probation	1,165
Other Services	4,867
Recreation, culture and health	1,880
	61,223

Note: In the face of rate-capping and a 'recalcitrant government' (Leader's Annual Report) 1985/86 was to be a year of financial stringency with the Consumer Protection Department's budget being cut by 10% on 1984/85 levels

Appendix 5.8   *Rutshire County Council Consumer Protection Department Budget for 1984/85*

£	
£1,750,000	Wages and staff development costs (138 personnel)[1]
5,000	Capital expenditure (new Weights and Measures testing equipment)
250,000	Rent, rates, heating, lighting and upkeep of premises (4 divisional offices, 4 consumer advice centres, 1 central office)
10,000	'Test' purchases of products and services to ensure legal weights, descriptions, fitness for purpose, etc
69,000	Miscellaneous purchases, PR: professional advice, etc £10,000 per division + £19,000 central 'overall' fund

£2,084,000

(1)   2 Weights and Measures Inspectors, 2 Consumer Advisers, 1 Consumer Credit Officer and 1 Admin Assistant had resigned within the last two months of the year

Appendix 5.9   *Manpower Statement*

The table below shows the overall number of personnel employed on services wholly or partly financed by the County Council on 31 March 1985 as compared to 10 March 1984

Committee or Service	In Post 10 Mar. 84	In Post 31 Mar. 85
Consumer protection		
APT&C[1]	128	122
Manual	10	10
	138	132
Environment		
APT&C	116	118
Manual	146	146
	262	264
Fire service		
Uniformed and retained fireman	1,277	1,267
APT&C	69	66
Manual	111	105
	1,457	1,438
Highways		
APT&C	955	909
Manual	1,210	1,163
	2,165	2,072
Passenger transport		
SYPTE Manual	4,556	4,353
SYPTE Non-manual	775	776
	5,331	5,129
Planning and architecture		
APT&C	155	143
Police[2]		
APT&C	471	477
Manual	272	273
School crossing patrols	570	566
	4,239	4,243
Prosecuting solicitors		
APT&C	68	65

Committee or Service	In Post 10 Mar. 84	In Post 31 Mar. 85
Policy and other services		
Administration – APT&C	207	198
– Manual	94	92
Treasurers – APT&C	268	243
	569	533
Probation	389	456
Recreation, culture and Health		
APT&C	51	56
Manual	28	31
	79	87

(1)   APT&C – Administrative, Professional, Technical and Clerical Staff
(2)   Police Uniformed Personnel are not employees of the County Council

6·Silver Wheels Ltd

Bill Richardson and John Patterson

This case study is based on the general experience of the authors.

Scene 1

Silver Wheels Ltd, is a small, family-owned coach travel business. Founded at the turn of the century by the present owners' grandparents the concern had grown from a horse and cart operation to a 32-bus operation by 1953 when it became incorporated as a limited company.

In 1984, however, the trading situation was giving one of the directors, George Allen, cause for concern. 'The trouble is' said George, who had called a directors' meeting, 'our trading environment has changed without our really noticing it. Just after the war, in our heyday, competition wasn't so fierce. There weren't so many small operators in the area and the big boys like Wallace Arnold, National Travel and Counties Travel served the main towns and left us to mop up in our own localities. Nowadays every village seems to have its own operator and the major operators have become more competitive every year.

'We've lived – and worked – through the birth and boom of extended British holidays and tours. We still do good business in this market but increasingly the public are looking to holiday abroad. They expect *luxury* travel, too, and you know that we've been hard pressed in recent years to maintain a reasonably modern fleet. At the same time customers are shopping around for price as well as quality and John will confirm that his quotations are often rejected by customers who've had better offers elsewhere.

'This year's balance sheet reflects the worsening profit situation and (for me this is the greatest worry) we all know that the Government's de-licensing legislation takes effect next year. The protection we've enjoyed on our licensed excursion and tours routes goes by the board next year. We will be involved in a free for all and the local competition has been wetting its lips in preparation for an all-out attack on our established routes next year.

'In short, I'm suggesting that we've a serious situation on our hands. We've got to use a different approach to running this business. It's no use burying our heads and relying on hard work to make a living. None of us is getting any younger and I'm afraid that hard work alone is no longer a guarantee of success.

'One last thing; the four of us each earned £5,800 last year. In 1983, for the work and responsibility we incur, that really is "peanuts" – and there hasn't been a dividend declared in years. I'm nearly 60 and you three aren't too far behind me. It's time we had a bit more to show for all the work and worry we've put in over the years.

'I've brought some financial information relating to our operations and – don't ask me how – I've managed to get hold of this year's accounts for Roadster Ltd (see Appendix 6.1). I think some of the figures in their accounts will surprise us and – importantly – help us to start thinking about where we are and where we want to be. I'd like to think we could start by improving the age of our fleet but you know we have consistently strained our overdraft limit of £15,000 over the past five years. The only way we've managed to balance our cash flow position has been through buying cheaper and older replacement coaches than we would otherwise have preferred.'

Scene 2   (around the same time as Scene 1)

Roadster Ltd is a small family-owned coach business presently operated by Hector Shaw (the son of the firm's founder) and Hector's son, Mark. The following text is extracts of a conversation which took place during a coffee break in the small booking office located at Roadster's premises.

Hector: 'Early bookings suggest that our licensed tours will do OK again this year and the new private hire contracts we secured during the off season should help.'

Mark: 'Yes. If the weather is kind to us this year and helps us do well with the day and weekend work we should at least maintain last year's level of profit performance. But what about the longer term, Dad? You're 64 next month. Maybe it's time you were taking things easier. The signs are that times are going to get tougher in this industry.'

Hector: 'There's plenty of life left yet. Don't worry about me. I reckon that we're up to the new challenges. This firm grew up in a deregulated environment. We still get 60% of our business in the freely competitive private hire sector and we have a good name. I think we can more than hold our own against the smaller independent opposition. They'll learn during the next couple of years that filling holiday coaches and day trips depends upon more than simply advertising a destination in the local papers.'

Mark: 'Yes, but we can't "magic" a bigger community. There are only so many people to go round – and the big boys are becoming more professional and aggressive. This year we really have to look after our customers and to keep developing new private hire links . . .'

Hector: 'We would do a lot better, too, if we could get some cooperation from Counties Travel and Silver Wheels. It breaks my heart to see coaches from each organisation setting off to the same destination on the same day, each only one third full.'

Mark: 'Yes, but you know I tried to get some collusion over who goes where and when. I'm sure with that sort of arrangement we could maintain turnover and reduce running costs by 10% or more. As it is, with all the independents trying to get a piece of the action things aren't likely to get any better. The drivers should be more settled, though, since we introduced the same wage rates as Counties Travel back at the beginning of 1983.'

Hector: 'We have a number of things going for us. I think it was an astute move on my part, giving you full rein when I reached 60. Since then I've watched the bank balance move slowly and surely from zero to around £20,000. Profits have improved and, in terms of British holidays and excursions, our fleet is the best around here.'

Scene 3 (around the same time as Scenes 1 and 2)

(The Managing Director's office – Counties Travel Ltd)

The Managing Director: 'Next year we lose the virtual monopoly we've held in this area so far as our licensed tours and excursion routes are concerned. Further, since we brought the Ravensthorpe to Anston services from Silver Wheels some years ago we have been the only operator undertaking stage carriage services but I confidently expect that the licensed protection we enjoy in this type of work will be removed by the present Government within the next three years. These licensed operations presently account for 20% and 40% of our total turnover, respectively. The remainder, as you know is roughly comprised of 30% private hire and 10% works contracts. If Government 'rate-capping' pressure gets any stronger I also suspect that we will be saying goodbye to the subsidies we receive from the County Council in return for our complying with their cheap fares policy. For the past 10 years we have had things relatively easy. We've allowed a lot of "slack" to creep into our systems and we've not been mindful enough of the need to make useful profits. We have to change. On the one hand we will face increased local competition in our tours, excursions and stage carriage markets. On the other hand we can expect the more widely drawn companies of about our own size (120 buses/coaches) to re-route their British and Continental coach holidays to pick up in Anston. Of course, we in turn, can take the opportunity to market our own services in their areas. Whichever way we look at today's situation, however, we can see the need to change our presently over-bureaucratic and introverted methods of organising and operating.

'We also have to be alert to new opportunities. In this context I have two potential investment opportunities in mind at the moment. I'd appreciate your taking a look at them . . .

'You all know Silver Wheels and Roadster – two of our longer-standing competitors. I think they might be ripe for takeover. They are the only operators around here (us apart) to hold any licences for excursions and tours. While they have never been big enough to really bother us they do, undoubtedly, take some of our business. Like us, they maintain a strong presence locally through being seen, through their uses of local shops as booking agents, and through their network of well-established passenger picking up points. We have always maintained contact with both sets of directors – I had occasion to discuss some matters with them, separately, only last week.

'George Allen, particularly, is concerned about Silver Wheels' position these days. All the directors are in their mid to late 50s, I guess, and while they are good 'old school' travel industry types I don't think they are up to handling effectively today's environments. In their early days I suppose they had thought that they were building up a viable business for their children but (quite sensibly, perhaps) it seems that the kids have moved on to greener occupational pastures. I think they might be ready to sell – if we are willing to buy. There might be some minor integration problems. Their coaches aren't up to our standards and I think their staff are on wage scales about 10% below ours. There might also, of course, be some advantages . . .

'Roadster is, in many ways, a similar set-up to Silver Wheels. This time, however, we'd be dealing with old Hector Shaw and his son, Mark. They are altogether sharper – Mark particularly is really on the ball. Hector is in his 60s though and the right sort of deal might tempt them to sell.

'I have copies of Roadster and Silver Wheels' accounts (see Appendix 6.1) and I also have some industry average performance ratios (see Appendix 6.2). I'd like us to give some early thought to the financial and organisational issues involved in these potential acquisition strategies.'

Appendix 6.1 *Trading and Profit and Loss Account*

| | Silver Wheels Ltd Years ended 31 Dec. 1982/83 | | Roadster Travel Ltd 31 Dec. 83 |
	1982	1983	1983
Earnings	146,556	159,475	120,343
Deduct cost of earnings:			
Wages and National Insurance	44,082	47,829	28,963
Petrol, diesel, oil	30,749	33,017	18,206
Tyres	3,906	4,319	2,126
Spares	17,157	18,967	7,851
Parking fees/Drivers' subsistence	3,648	3,480	3,241

Appendix 6.1 (Continued)

	Silver Wheels Ltd 1982	Silver Wheels Ltd 1983	Roadster Ltd 1983
Coaches hired in	9,051	9,106	2,634
Licences	1,314	2,090	1,200
Insurances	4,472	4,440	3,140
Stock – Opening	5,483	7,411	2,001
	119,862	130,659	69,362
Less Closing stock	7,411	8,076	2,224
	112,451	122,583	67,138
Gross profit	34,105	36,892	53,205
Add Other income:			
Bank interest	8	28	–
Profit on sales of vehicles	9,327	7,484	15,000
	43,440	44,404	68,205
Deduct:			
Admin expenses			
Directors' remuneration	9,323	11,604	21,000
Postage and telephone	1,360	1,783	1,236
Painting and advertising	1,633	2,576	2,240
Audit charges	735	1,000	550
Subscriptions	98	155	–
Legal and professional charges	–	195	–
General expenses	–	–	1,000
Establishment charges			
Rates	1,291	1,569	1,400
Light and heat	1,876	2,765	2,165
Repairs and renewals	285	1,641	1,600
Financial expenses			
Bank charges	1,500	1,085	474
Discounts allowed to customers	1,539	1,641	431
HP interest	–	–	500
Depreciation			
Motor vehicles	12,818	13,606	16,100
Petrol pumps	3	3	–
Machinery	1	1	–
	32,462	39,624	48,696
Net profit	10,978	4,780	19,509

Additional Financial Information

1 Silver Wheels wages include £11,604 (1983) for two of the four directors (these two are employed primarily as coach drivers rather than administrators).

2 Coaches are 'hired in' from other operators to cover excess demand in busy periods.

3   Profits on sales of vehicles is due largely to over depreciation in previous years.

4   HP interest (see Roadster account) has accrued, following the purchase, from another operator, of a coach which was subject to an HP agreement.

5   Previous Silver Wheels net profits have been £14,036 (1978); £20,501 (1979); £16,402 (1980); £18,791 (1981).

	Silver Wheels Ltd Balance sheet 31 Dec. 83		Roadster Ltd Balance sheet 31 Dec. 83	
Fixed assets				
Land and building (at cost 1953)	8,217		15,000 (1958)	
Petrol pumps	26		–	
Plant	2		–	
Loose tools	1,156		–	
Fixtures and fittings	592		1,212	
Motor vehicles	55,896		80,000	
		65,889		96,212
Current assets				
Stock	8,076		2,224	
Debts and prepayments	25,541		10,211	
Cash and bank balance	2,764		19,326	
	36,381		30,761	
Current liabilities				
Creditors	23,501		15,932	
Bank overdraft	14,643		–	
Finance company loan	–		5,000	
Directors current accounts	13,770		35,000	
	51,914	(15,533)	55,932	(24,171)
		50,356		72,041
Share capital		1,000		10,000
Retained earnings		45,759		62,041
Capital Reserve		3,597		–
		50,356		72,041

Additional Balance Sheet Information
1   Land and buildings (for both organisations) now stand at £60,000 (current valuations) although Silver Wheels has three times the area of land (much of it unused) and bigger garage and office blocks.

2   Silver Wheels has 10 Bedford/Plaxton coaches; the newest 5 years old, the oldest 10 years old.

3   Roadster has 6 Bedford/Plaxton coaches; the newest 2 years old, the oldest 5 years old.

4   Directors' current accounts are composed of loans made to the companies, over the years, by the directors.

5   Stock consists of petrol, diesel, oil, tyres and spares.

Other generally known information
1   Silver Wheels has a particularly good (price-wise) contract for petrol, diesel and oil.

2   Roadster's two directors are concerned mainly with planning and administration.

3   Silver Wheels earns revenue from the following sources:

★ Works contracts (NCB, local factories, etc.) and school services (2 coaches are employed 5 days per week on these services)

★ Day, weekend and extended British excursions, tours and holidays. Licensed (rather than private hire) operations in these areas accounted for approximately 30% of turnover. However, profit contribution breakdowns have never been attempted.

4   Roadster has almost identical markets except that it does not operate any works or school contracts.

Appendix 6.2   *Some Industry Performance Standards*

Current ratio	1.1
Gearing	50%
Interest cover ratio	11.0
Fixed charge cover ratio	5.0
Stock control	25
Permanent asset turnover ratio	2.0
ROCE	10%
ROS	12%
ROE	44%
Gross profit margin	35%
Fuel to earnings	17%
Average seating capacity full (Licensed excursions, tours and holidays)	80%
Admin expenses to sales	20%

Appendix 6.3   *Counties Travel, Silver Wheels and Roadster*
Geographical Relationship

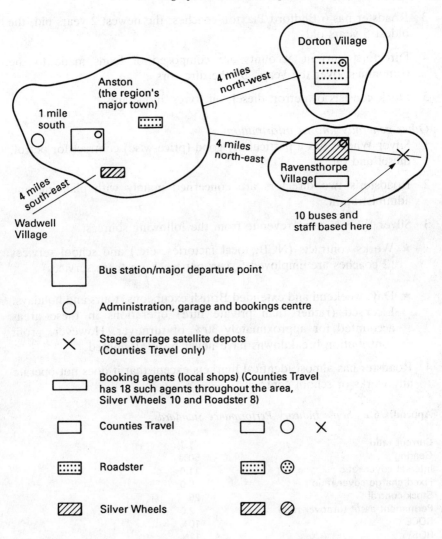

	Bus station/major departure point
○	Administration, garage and bookings centre
×	Stage carriage satellite depots (Counties Travel only)
	Booking agents (local shops) (Counties Travel has 18 such agents throughout the area, Silver Wheels 10 and Roadster 8)

▭	Counties Travel	▭	○	×
▦	Roadster	▦	⊛
▨	Silver Wheels	▨	⊘

Appendix 6.4   *Counties Travel – 1984 Expenditure Budget for*
Satellite Bus Depot at Ravensthorpe

	£
Wages and salaries	66,000
Petrol, diesel and oil	40,000
Spares and repairs	20,000
Licences and insurance	7,000
Miscellaneous	2,500
Telephone	1,000

Rates	
Light and heat	2,000
	4,000
	£142,500

Value of land and premises £40,000 (recent internal evaluation)

Salaries/wages:	£
Depot Manager	
Foreman/Assistant Manager	10,000
Drivers (per driver)	7,500
	5,800

7·High Street Electricals plc

Bill Richardson

This case study is intended as an aid to class discussion, rather than as a comment on the handling of a business situation.

The 1982 position

'As we approached the task of turning the company around we could see clearly a number of major problems that required urgent attention. They were all symptoms of the general malaise of a national organisation being run in an introverted, traditional, family way.'

In 1982 it was obvious to the newly incumbent management team at High Street Electricals plc (HSE) that drastic changes were required. The situation was daunting. The 1982 annual accounts showed losses of almost £4m against turnover of £42m. Massive cash injections were also needed urgently. Net debts consistently running around £10m had been a constant headache and had generated crippling interest charges.

Despite interventions by the Office of Fair Trading back in 1978 when the company had demanded unauthorised rental charge increases in breach of contracts, customer relations and practices had not improved. The organisation wasn't anti-social so much as apathetic to the needs and demands of its external stakeholders. Success achieved in the 'heady' days of 'Barberism' and TV sales booms had bred false confidence. The organisation was no longer effective at earning a living from an increasingly turbulent, hostile and mature market. (Information on market shares and conditions can be gleaned from the text and from Appendices 7.1 and 7.2.)

Inside the organisation, further significant problems were apparent. Control was poor. Branch managers were effectively running, in their own way, their particular business units. Senior and middle management didn't talk much to each other. Sales staff and service departments did not always cooperate. Motivation was low. Resources with which to instigate changes were patently scarce. Earlier successes had facilitated and disguised the building up of inefficiencies within the organisation.

The new management

Since its foundation in 1897 HSE had been owned and managed by members of the Jameson family. The crises of the late 1970s and early 1980s, however, had resulted in the installation of a new chairman, John Fellows (who brought with him a useful track record with a variety of electrical industry companies) and a new managing director, David Monks. David Monks had previously been employed by HSE competitor (Rumbelows Ltd). In his early 40s he was perceived to have the necessary marketing and leadership qualities to lead the HSE 'turnaround'. David recruited former Rumbelow colleagues Simon Sparkes, Andrew Field-send and Peter Jordan to head the organisation's finance, operating systems and marketing functions, respectively. Together with Roy Sunders, a long-serving HSE executive, this group of people comprised the HSE top strategic team. Together they quickly set about remedying the problems facing HSE.

Product/market operations

Rent or sell?

A root problem for the company was provided by its major product/market strategy – TV (and other electrical goods) *rentals* . . .

'Our branch managers were geared towards pushing *new* rental agreements with *old* customers. New sets were going out over longer periods for the same weekly rental payments. All we were getting in return for the new and costly sets were the old secondhand ones. We also felt that the market was moving against rentals generally and that before long there would be room for perhaps only two major rental companies. Recent mergers tend to have confirmed our judgement of that time.'

A new strategy was implemented. HSE needed to become a *retailer* – not a *renter*. By 1985 rental contribution to turnover was down from 50% to less than 10%. Rental remains available in some branches but where possible staff now *sell* goods on cash or credit terms. The sale of a portfolio of rental accounts in 1982 (to VisionHire for £4m cash) fitted the new strategic direction and provided a vital injection of liquidity.

Geographic areas of operation and distribution

Forty HSE stores were disposed of (all below Oxford) with the intention of 'reducing borrowings (£4m sales price), stabilising trade and operating in a tight geographical area' (Chairman's Report, 1982). A sprinkling of southern stores has been maintained to preserve a national image (in 1986 HSE was promoting itself as 'Britain's biggest electrical independent'). Strong market position, however, is enjoyed only in HSE's home county.

A total of around 100 branches is maintained but within this total figure relocation policies mean that new branches are regularly replacing older ones . . .

'Many of our branches just weren't big enough to stock the items we wanted to sell. We have been disposing of our smaller, village premises as suitable alternative sites – and the necessary finance – have become available. (Although new sites are leased it still costs around £400,000 to open a large store.) We have been opening bigger and better town centre branches and "out of town" superstores.'

Recent superstore openings had been made at Leicester, Buxton and, for the first time in Lancashire, at Bolton.

A systematic refurbishment programme was also implemented. The aim here was to lift the image of the company into the 1980s and 1990s through a more futuristically designed sales outlet, utilising a distinctive colour scheme and HSE 'uniformed' staff. Visits around the HSE chain in 1987 confirmed this transitionary position. Older outlets were either in the process of, or getting ready for, their refits and alignment with the modern 'HSE – buy better electric' image (and away from their traditional 'HSE – friend of the family' stance).

Products and buying policies

HSE stocks a range of popular 'brown' and 'white' goods (see, for example, the products listed in Appendix 7.3) . . . 'We used to have to try and sell a load of garbage, really', explained one branch manager. 'I think that top management felt that they couldn't get the terms they wanted from the popular manufacturers. It's different now though. We stock what the customers want – the better quality merchandise – and we often knock the spots off competition in price terms. Yesterday I took a walk around a local department store that always seemed to have *the* merchandise. We now match them product for product and can beat them easily on price. Our buyers check things out well and the directors personally inspect new lines before they are introduced . . . We also have fewer problems with defective goods. It makes sense, I suppose. Some years ago when we also sold lower-priced furniture we used to have even more problems with product quality and customer complaints'.

David Monks commented on the product/buying situation . . . 'Buying policies were woefully inadequate. Personal contacts between directors and suppliers counted far more than quality or customer appeal product characteristics. The company was an "easy touch" for some manufacturers and it had been overbuying.' Everyone seemed in accord with the new move towards this acquisition and sale of popular branded goods. The more recent moves of a major (and market leader) competitor – Dixons – towards the supply of its own brands was, however, already being viewed with some apprehension. Dixon's ability to buy in huge quantities and then sell at very low prices was also giving cause for concern. The availability of credit and extended warranty cover facilities were important supplements to the goods on offer for sale.

Pricing

The electrical goods retailing industry exhibits many of the economist's perfect market characteristics. Numerous sellers operating in the confined areas of high streets offer selections of largely homogeneous products. The buying public thus has the opportunity to shop around for the best deal. HSE, like many leading competitors offer a 'we'll match any competitor's price' guarantee. As one middle manager explained . . . '25 years ago the HSE salesmen were "kings" around here. Our doorstep selling approach of those times brought new consumer goods to a captive audience. There is no longer such a thing as a HSE customer, however. We now have to attract customers anew – every time they buy. This is all about presentation, service and, particularly, price'.

An internal newsheet *Livewire* keeps staff uptodate on price and other variations in the market-place (staff phone in relevant information as it appears). Further, staff regularly conduct their own 'espionage' forays in their sales territories. Branch managers hold discretion to match any competitive price offer.

Promotion

The location of sales outlets, their overall ambience and internal display modes were seen as important forms of promotion. More overt promotional media included local newspapers and window and in-store display areas. Weekly information bulletins from Head Office provided publicity material and instructions on how to implement the material in order to ensure a uniform approach to publicity and the maintenance of the desired HSE image.

Customer service

Branch managers changed the layout of their stores periodically and kept in mind the need to create 'one big cohesive sales unit' where customers could see all parts of the store (and all ranges of goods on offer) from any position therein. While staff agreed that 'you have to "hit" the customer while he is in or he'll leave and buy the same merchandise across the road', nevertheless, they were increasingly aware of the need to be courteous, friendly and professional in order to differentiate the organisation, particularly from some of its bigger, more impersonal, 'cash and carry' type competitors. Branch managers were particularly proud of the service back-up HSE provided . . . 'Sales and Service didn't get on at one time. They thought we were pests and we thought they were unhelpful. Things have changed, thank goodness. We are encouraged to get together more – at training sessions and meetings, or just simply during the working day. We're continually in touch and we help each other. They are quick, flexible and efficient and, unlike many of our competitors who rely on outside service organisations, they're *our own*'.

Customer care

Appendix 7.4 shows complaints statistics obtained from HSE's home authority trading standards department. Interpretation of complaints statistics is recognised as being fraught with difficulties. However, the following points in connection with HSE's customer complaints situation are worth making:

1   In general terms, complaints against HSE have been falling since 1979 while turnover has remained constant (at least in value terms) and has, since 1982, been generated predominantly in the home authority area.

2   HSE complaint trends compare favourably with general complaint trends over electrical goods.

3   Staff from the local authority confirm that . . . 'HSE now creates much less work for us than used to be the case' and that, 'HSE's central customer relations department is very useful on those occasions when we remain in dispute with branch managers'.

4   Price complaints as a proportion of total complaints have reduced considerably, perhaps as a consequence of the changed product/market strategy. Trading Standards staff regularly commented that . . . 'We used to have problems sorting out rental payments' and (by way of further comment on the effect product/market strategies can have on complaint situations) . . . 'Going even further back we used to have lots of problems over furniture complaints'.

5   Merchantable quality problems remain consistently the biggest source of complaints. HSE staff feel that this problem is not totally within their control because: they do not have a sufficiently strong bargaining position with which to enforce change from the manufacturers – costs incurred in improving manufacturer's product quality capabilities would outweigh the benefits, particularly as any improvements would automatically benefit those competitors who share the same manufacturers.

The organisation therefore adopts a 'cure' rather than 'prevention' approach to product quality failure by:

1   Offering extended warranty cover schemes (see Appendix 7.3)

2   Relying on 'sensible' relationships with suppliers to cater for the return, repair or replacement of rogue products (cash refunds remain the exception rather than the rule in faulty product situations)

3   The provision of efficient, courteous and friendly attention to customers with problems

4   The installation of an improved central consumer care department

5   The provision of a speedy collection and repair service

6   Reliance on improving quality standards (many traditional electrical goods do enjoy improving performance records, generally).

Finance

An early problem was due to the Jamesons not wanting to invest further in HSE – or lose control to outside investors.

Finance has remained a constant problem. Despite the sales of a large portfolio of customer rental accounts and the sale of one third of HSE's branch outlets and the raising of a £2.36m rights issue in 1985 a £10m annual average net debt and attendant interest charges has been wrestled with continually during the period. Profitability has remained elusive and earnings per share/dividend performance has been poor. Appendix 7.5 charts some financial performance indicators since 1979. During this period, too, HSE has survived a major takeover bid by Philips, the electrical giant, and has lived with the rumour of further takeover attempts.

Inside the organisation

The problems facing David Monks and his top team weren't only over external developments. The 'new look' HSE required internal changes, too. The major impetus for this change had to come from David and his aides . . .

'The old management were OK – George Jameson was a real gentleman – but they tended to visit only the "old guard" – staff whom they knew well. To the rest of us they were unapproachable, really. Now the new management team seem to get everywhere – they just call and talk to *anybody*. You can give them your honest opinion, too. I wouldn't have dared go against the views of the old management. We've also started bi-monthly meetings (we hire some hotel room) which David Monks chairs. Those are really good for passing information and airing views. You come out of them really buzzing . . .'

'I am impressed with their sharpness of mind. You talk to them and they don't take notes, or anything, but two or three days later you get a memo which directly covers the issues that you raised. I suggested to

Mr Sparkes that we could reschedule our 'customers in arrears' visits more efficiently. A couple of days later he wrote to say we'd adopted my ideas. Things are working much better there now. They gave me a small bonus, too.'

'You visit head office and you look out for Mr Monks' door. It is almost always open. I could pick up the phone here and now and speak to him directly. Which other major company in this field has such direct links between branch staff and the top man? . . .'

'He gets involved with customers, quite often taking their telephone complaints personally. I'm not sure that the old team knew what customers were. Also we used to have to follow fixed rules, but one of the worst things you can do is to quote rules at a complaining customer. Each one needs to be treated separately and, if necessary, uniquely . . .'

'I think we needed somebody to look at things in a cool, professional way. The new management team have done this.'

David Monks is aware of the need to create team spirit . . . 'create a good team and the *team* will resolve problems'. His assertion that the new style of management at HSE is 'simply a new post-war Christian approach to management' needs to be viewed, however, in the context of his team's record on the making of tough decisions and the taking of 'hard lines' on certain issues . . .

'Basically you've got to tell everyone what is expected of them . . .' and, . . . 'We're looking for "sparkle" in this organisation. We are getting there but it hasn't been easy. We've had to work hard at getting people talking to each other and working together. Many suffered culture shock, too, when they were required to sell something other than a Hoover product. We had to train staff to sell a range of different products. Also we had no 25's to 35's in the organisation. All the talent had moved out. We've reintroduced the younger element – largely through internal development and promotions. Just about all the old executives have gone voluntarily. Most were just not up to it, although some had potential and will undoubtedly be better now that they have gained experience of more professional approaches elsewhere.'

Younger, early 30's, managers are now enjoying the positions that might only have been available to them in their late 40's.

'. . . Also, we had to get people *doing* things. For example, the top executive meetings used to be simply an easy afternoon's "get together". Now I take notes, we agree points of action and use the sessions as springboards for doing things . . . At one stage we did get into harmful "scoring points" game with the unions. In the end we just had to be "tough skinned" and carry on with our plans.'

A major impetus towards improved organisational performance has been the introduction of a new £400,000 computerised control system. Improvements in credit and stock control have resulted. It has also helped create less overt, but nevertheless real, benefits associated with improved staff motivation. Inside the organisation the setting of, and speedy performance feedback on, sales targets has fixed organisation attention on the important objectives of increased turnover and profitability.

'We are involved in what I'd call friendly competition with other branches. We know how well everybody is doing. For example, we are currently third in the league behind Leicester and Buxton. But we've only been open at this site for the past six months. We'll catch them . . .'

'The bonus is useful, of course, but this is the real "turn on". Charting ourselves against targets each week is a great motivator in itself . . .'

'The whole mood of the branch depends upon how Monday's print-outs of the previous week's figures compare with our targets. If they are up, so are we. If they're down we have to shake ourselves out of despondency by discussing why they are down and how we are going to get back on schedule . . .'

Another successful manager, however, commented on some of the more difficult aspects of the system . . . 'It's like any business, I suppose. The better you do the better they want you to do. I've done well and so my targets are a lot higher than many of my colleagues. I've got to meet the new targets or my personal earnings will suffer – but there's a limit to the growth. I have eight major competitors within half a mile of this branch. We are still suffering the effects of the miners' strike and the County Council has, of course, just been abolished. The end of council subsidised bus fares means that travelling costs around here have gone up three or fourfold. People aren't coming into town as much as they used to. The pressure is always on.'

Despite the many changes successfully achieved over the past few years at HSE, conditions, then, remain difficult. David Monks appreciates that the quest for safety and growth is an enduring one and that success is relative – it needs to be measured in terms of the internal and external opportunities and constraints which are major factors in the success equation. He remains cautiously optimistic . . . 'We are getting there. The organisation now has "sparkle". Turnover is up 6% on last year despite increased competition. We have achieved breakeven twice (better than the £4m loss situation we inherited). We are shaking off the shackles of our rental policy – and we are, of course, still in work. We must now push on for greater profitability'.

David's hope must be for the realisation of a young, newly promoted manager's enthusiastic claim . . . 'I've never been so excited and proud about the job and the organisation. The "new HSE" is where it's at. We're the force in electrical retailing'.

Appendix 7.1 *Typical media extracts on the electrical goods retail trade 1984–86*

(A) A furious row erupted yesterday over the news that Granada Group has made a conditional agreement to buy the Comet elec-

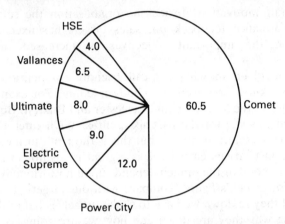

How Comet dominates out-of-town retailing

trical retailing group should Dixons win its unwanted takeover bid for Woolworth. Since its takeover of Rediffusion in 1984, for £120m, Granada TV rental has become the biggest in the TV rental business with 650 high street outlets. Last year it tested the sale of manufacturer-branded goods in its Scottish shops and found that one third of revenue was generated by retail, without significant adverse impact on the rental business. As a result, by the end of this year it is planned that two thirds of Granada's shops will offer TVs for sale and thus double its potential market. Comet is the leading name in the edge of town section, operating 60% of the UK outlets in this sector. Woolworth's director Mr Nigel Whittaker called the offer 'ludicrous' and suggested that if Alex Bernstein at Granada were to get Comet at the price Mr Kalas has suggested he would be 'laughing all the way to the bank'.

(B)   HSE the northern electrical goods group and the Leeds chain Vallances are among the first set of retailers nationally to sell Sir Clive Sinclair's controversial battery-powered vehicle, the C5. The vehicle will be on display in some 22 of HSE's stores and test drives are planned in the car-parks of the chain's superstores. For HSE, the massive publicity for the C5 is well timed to fit in with its new superstore strategy, and yesterday – the first day when the C5 was put up for sale in HSE outlets – was also the first day of the group's shareholders meeting to approve a £2.36 million rights issue, the proceeds of which are to go towards developing superstore sites. David Monks, HSE's managing director, described the C5 development as 'exciting' but would not say how many of the vehicles, which retail at £399.00 each, were in stock.

(C)   HSE, the white and brown goods retailer, is raising £2.36m fresh capital with a rights issue of 7% convertible preference shares.

Managing Director David Monks who arrived at lossmaker HSE from Rumbelows in May 1982, said yesterday the money would be used to implement a five-year plan which would see four superstore, edge of town outlets, open each year while smaller high street sites (HSE has 96 of these) would be updated and closely scrutinised for profitability. The fresh capital will also go towards a computerised sales system. Mr Monks says that, currently some ten days could lapse between sales figures being transmitted, so that outlets ran out of stock.

Patient HSE shareholders must be wondering when HSE will turn around. Yesterday's announcement was accompanied by a gloomy forecast that the year to March would see losses of not more than £75,000. This is against a £35,000 profit last time. HSE put the blame on competitive trading, recent interest rate rises and the continuing miners' strike which, it says, has cost the group £400,000 profit in the current year. No dividend has been paid for the past three years but the board will recommend a 2.5p net for the year to March 1986.

(D)   Telefusion, the Blackpool TV rental and electrical goods retailer, yesterday produced interim results which underline the need for its decision to combine both businesses and rename all its stores Connect. The relaunch of its 200 or more stores in the new colours cost £900,000 up to October, and this, along with a £5m downturn in turnover and severe problems in the high street business before the name change brought about a pre-tax loss of £367,000 against a £1.25m profit last time.

(E)   Dixons, the camera to hi-fi group newly expanded after its bitter Curry takeover coup, yesterday sold something few people realised it had – snuff. Permaflex is a Dixon subsidiary and is the subject of a management buy-out. Eleven months on, the Dixons/Currys operation is widely regarded in the City as the perfect double act. Already market leaders in camera sales, the new 800 store operation will soon be selling one in four of the brown goods sold in the UK. Combined sales and profit are well in excess of the sum of previous individual performance figures. Dixons has recently sold 210,000 TV rental contracts (acquired from Currys). Dixons' view is that selling and renting sets should not be carried out by the same outlets.

Dixons' retail policies have translated into useful financial performances. Earnings per share are up from 19.5p in 1982 to 35.8p in 1985. Share prices (annual averages) have moved from £2.08 in 1982 to £7.50 in 1985. Turnover and profits of £117 million and £6 million respectively grew to £275 million and £22 million, respectively, over the same period.

(F)   The Japanese electronics industry is set to plunge the audio market
into another revolutionary phase that threatens to kill off the
compact disc market before development costs have been
recovered. The newcomer is the digital audio tape (dat). Deliveries
of compact disc equipment to trade outlets rose to 147,000 units last
year compared with 17,000 in 1983. The total is expected to reach
half a million this year. The music industry gives a warning that
'if DAT is allowed to arrive on the market in an untimely and
disorderly appearance, it might be the final blow to the recording
industry'.

Sales of electronic home entertainment products have dropped
by £500,000 in the past two years. The industry is 'currently
ploughing a furrow between the crests of product development'.
Home computer and video sales have levelled off while the development of products which link with each other will not reach the
market before the 1990s. The sectors most likely to grow are
television sets, video cameras and in-car entertainment. The home
computer market appears to be at saturation point. Sales in the
small audio market – radios, recorders and walkmen – peaked in
1984.

Appendix 7.2   *Business Monitor Statistics*

Retail sales (£ million)

	1980	1982	1984
Photographic and optical goods	401	464	434
Audio visual equipment hire and relay	962	1125	1182

Appendix 7.3 *H.S.E. Proposal Form*

DIS | 115 | Extended Warranty covers new products only and must be applied for within 30 days from the date of purchase as new

2039 | 03 | Title   Initials   Surname

Name

Address

Postcode

Date of Purchase

Make

Model   Purchase Price £

THE ORIGINAL MANUFACTURER'S GUARANTEE (ONE YEAR UNLESS OTHERWISE STATED) COMMENCING AT DATE OF PURCHASE EXTENDED TO 5 YEARS IN ALL.
(Please place a cross in one box only.)

		Premium				Premium
Monochrome TV	1	☐ £13.49	Audio Equipment and Colour			
Colour TV	2	☐ £37.99	Television up to 20" combined	10	☐ £59.99
Colour TV, 2 year					
Manufacturers Guarantee	3	☐ £31.99	Twin Tub	11	☐ £38.99
Laser Video	4	☐ £79.99	Tumble Dryer	12	☐ £33.99
Video Disc		☐ £39.99	Freezer or Fridge Freezer	13	☐ £19.99
Digital Audio or Compact Disc	5	☐ £64.99	Freezer or Fridge Freezer with		
Audio Equipment up to £150	6	☐ £23.99	Food Spoilage limit £300	14	☐ £29.99
Audio Equipment £151 to £500	7	☐ £28.99	Refridgerator	15	☐ £17.99
Audio Equipment £501 to £1000	8	☐ £39.99	Microwave Oven up to £300	16	☐ £29.99
Audio Equipment and Colour			Microwave Oven over £300	17	☐ £29.99
Television up to 16" combined	9	☐ £59.99	Vacuum Cleaner	27	☐ £13.99

THE ORIGINAL MANUFACTURER'S ONE YEAR GUARANTEE COMMENCING AT DATE OF PURCHASE EXTENDED TO:–

		3 years in all		5 years in all
Home Computer up to £200				
Console only	18	☐ £22.99		
Video Cassette Recorder	19	☐ £49.99	23	☐ £97.99
Automatic Washing Machine	20	☐ £39.99	24	☐ £89.99
Automatic Washer Dryer	21	☐ £49.99	25	☐ £119.99
Dishwasher	22	☐ £34.99	26	☐ £79.99

FOR DEALER USE

Branch code
Cost centre

Staff No.

Please hand to shop staff who will issue you with a receipt or forward to H.S.E. "Supercover" Department, together with a copy of your sale receipt as proof of purchase.
Cheques should be made payable to:

Branch Name   Tog   Man   Model

5 | 4

N.B. the premiums shown for the periods of cover indicated apply until the 28th February 1986.

Credit Account Number   Cash Transaction

Appendix 7.4 *Electrical Goods and Consumer Complaints Statistics*

HSE Ltd: Annual complaints level (volume)

1979	1980	1981	1982	1983	1984
808	700	702	609	544	548

Source: Home Authority records of complaints registered at Consumer Advice centres

Industry complaint totals

1981	1982	1983	1984
3,956	4,300	5,105	5,027

Source: Home Authority records of complaints registered at Consumer Advice centres.

Appendix 7.5   *HSE Financial Performance Indicators*

Year	T/o	Pre-tax profit £ millions	Earnings per share	Gross dividend	Share price
1979	41.9	1.85	20p	2.5p	–
1980	44.3	0.91	14.9p	1.1p	–
1981	45.3	0.63	9.6p	1.6p	–
1982	42.4	−3.72	−71.5p	Nil	98p (lowest)
1983	40.6	−1.68	−18.8p	Nil	2.00 (highest)
1984	41.2	−0.05	0.7p	Nil	1.30 (average)
1985	46.3	+0.035	−1.2p	Nil	1.15 (lowest)
1986	55.0	+0.355	0.7p	2.5p	1.30 (average)

Extract from Chairman's statement year ended 1986:
'Price inflation in our sector remains low and total spending on electrical products increased by 9% on last year. Against this background our retail turnover performance has been commendable.'

HSE Ltd – Balance Sheets

	1981 £000	1982 £000	1985 £000	1986 £000
Fixed assets	25,468	23,790	17,063	14,034
Current assets				
Stocks	Not	Not	7,395	7,834
Debtors	Available	Available	6,442	6,451
Cash			118	142
	13,765	10,140	13,955	14,427
Current liabilities				
Creditors falling due within one year	(17,078)	(15,100)	(12,769)	(12,129)
Net current assets	(3,313)	(4,960)	1,186	2,298
Total assets *less* Current liabilities	22,155	18,830	18,249	16,332
Creditors due after more than one year	7,173	7,569	(5,421)	(3,366)
Deferred taxation			(75)	(75)
Net assets	14,982	11,261	12,753	12,891
Capital and reserves				
Called up share capital	1,316	1,316	3,918	3,918
Reserves	13,666	9,945	8,835	8,973
	14,982	11,261	12,753	12,891

8·Credit Grantors plc

Bill Richardson and Roy Richardson

This case study has been written from general experience and is intended as an aid to class discussion rather than as a comment on the effectiveness of the handling of a business situation.

Credit Grantors plc is a national finance company and member of the Finance Houses Association. It has a network of branches situated in many of the major towns and cities of England and generates its multi-million pounds annual turnover from the provision of finance in the form of secured and unsecured personal loans. Most business is effected through either of the following strategies:

1   Money shops, forming part of the town/city offices and dealing largely in loans to consumers.

2   Sales representatives ('fieldmen') who are each allocated a sales 'patch' and who generate business through personal selling. This business is, generally, of two types, ie consumer credit sold through trade customers, eg car sales outlets and industrial credit sold to business customers for industrial investment purposes, eg the purchase of machinery.

Performance appraisal/management by objectives

A variation of Management by Objectives is operated by the organisation. Before the start of each financial year individual 'fieldmen' meet with their branch manager and agree monthly targets for the next financial year. A starting point for negotiations is usually the performance achieved during the equivalent periods for the preceding year. Improved but realistic targets usually result from these meetings – it is generally agreed to be in the interests of both the sales representatives and the branch manager (who has to negotiate a branch target with his superior) to set targets which in the event will enable successful performance to be recorded. If agreement cannot be achieved, however, appeal can be made to the Area Manager. This procedure is rarely used.

Every month (about 10 days after the month end) a 'Fieldmen's Performance' list is received from Head Office showing each branch representative's performance against target for that month. Attached is a copy of such a document relating to performance of staff of Credit Grantor's Reading Branch. The practice is to exhibit the most recent list on the staff notice board.

During the course of each month Head Office also fowards 10-day and 20-day progress reports which the branch manager communicates to all staff (collectively in connection with total branch performance but individually at the initiation of the manager or the individual concerned in connection with individual performance). Staff tend to keep their own progress records as they transact business.

Bonuses attached to performance are not paid, although performance levels achieved do form part of the negotiation process at the end of each year when salary changes are negotiated by each representative and the Branch Manager. Representatives do not receive information on the amount of each other's salary and, between themselves, prefer to remain secretive on this issue.

Appendix 8.1   *Credit Grantors plc – Reading Office*

Performance Appraisal
Fieldmen's Performance to End August 1988

Name	Margin target £	Performance £	%
A C Crawshaw	5,833	9,662	166
D Fielding	5,600	8,067	143
R Brooksbanks	4,666	6,671	143
J Lodge	6,800	9,662	142
D V Raymond	6,800	7,414	109
L A Fields	6,333	6,429	102
N Kramer	6,250	5,911	95
R Butley	3,583	3,352	94
W Finsher	8,533	7,706	90
J K Robertson	7,500	6,155	82
D Newton	8,950	7,246	81
R I Jameson	9,483	7,382	78
J Cotton	6,675	4,401	66
V Spedding	8,750	5,371	61
R Johnson	6,990	4,010	57
L J Craven	6,250	3,070	49
P R Tait	6,670	2,237	34
J Lewis	6,670	2,124	32

9 · M & M Supplies Ltd

Bill Richardson

M & M Supplies Ltd had traded successfully for some years as a manufacturer supplying a variety of retail shops, cafes and restaurants, with its range of meat pies.

Recently M & M has been undertaking market research into the viability of some related diversification – the manufacture of a new prepacked, dehydrated, dog food product. Initial research results have been good and, using a prototype machine set up to fill bags to a weight of 500 grams each, 200 sample bags have been produced for use by the company's sales representatives.

However, a chance reference to the new product during a conversation with the company's solicitor culminated in Jane Chadwick, M & M's Managing Director, seeking advice from the local Weights and Measures Department. The inspector who subsequently called explained that the Weights and Measures Act 1979 applies legal controls to the weights of prepacked goods, and that for prepacked products bearing a marked weight of 500 grams (as per the new M & M product) the following legal rules apply:

1 The average of all such products produced should at least equal the marked weight.

2 Not more than 2 1/2% of the packages produced should weigh less than 485 grams.

3 No package should weigh less than 470 grams.

The inspector warned Mrs Chadwick that prosecutions were likely in cases where contraventions of the Act were discovered. He also took the opportunity of reminding Mrs Chadwick that the Food and Drugs Act 1955 might have relevance to the composition of M & M's traditional products (eg pork pies must contain at least 55% pork).

The inspector's visit had left Mrs Chadwick feeling decidedly uncomfortable. She felt that it was likely that the Weights and Measures Department would return at some future time to check the legality of M & M's operations and she was concerned that, despite every wish to operate within the law, poor quality control might cause violations.

Fear of prosecution, and any consequential fine and/or adverse publicity was uppermost in Mrs Chadwick's mind. However, this specific worry had also raised the question of quality control generally. Retail customers had complained over the fluctuating quality of products – in terms of weight, texture and taste. All too often it seemed (on reflection) the end consumer was less than satisfied with M & M's products.

Mrs Chadwick felt that quality failures were due, at least in part, to a mixture of some of the following factors:

★ different levels of skill, and care, on the part of production staff (55 people working on a two shift basis) and distribution staff (three van drivers and mates)

★ insufficiently 'tight' specifications on baking and machinery processes

★ fluctuating quality of ingredients from suppliers.

The week after the inspector's visit, Jane pondered over information provided by a quality control consultant. He had talked of 'assuming a normal distribution' and had promised to return with advice on the legality of the new dog food production process after having worked through the following 'limited sampling statistics'.

Weight of Samples (in grams)
5 consecutive bags taken randomly

Sample numbers	Mean of sample	Range of sample
1– 5	500.4	19
6–10	502.2	24
11–15	504.6	11
16–20	498.8	21
21–25	490.6	23
26–30	502.6	17

Jane was also looking at a number of quality based successful organisations (Pedigree Pet Foods; Jaguar Ltd; Greendale Electronics Ltd) in order to identify how her organisation might improve quality control via the development of a company-wide quality awareness. (See Appendices 9.1–9.3.)

Appendix 9.1 *Pedigree Petfoods*

'Inspection? That's the last thing we do!'
Leslie Simmens
Managing Director
Pedigree Petfoods

At Pedigree Petfoods, they believe that everyone is a quality controller – but the last thing they believe in is inspection. 'You can't inspect quality into a product'. They say inspection only weeds out the faults which should never have happened in the first place. It ignores what customers are getting and concentrates on what they are not getting. It makes you think of quality as a cost, not as a positive value.

At Pedigree, they prefer to put their efforts into 'forward control'. This means operating their plant so that mistakes don't happen – or, if they do, are immediately self-evident.

It means controlling every ingredient, every process, every machine – systematically, to the precise degree necessary to ensure the desired quality.

> *The precise dimensions of a can seam are vital to the production process*

It means training and motivating the workforce to understand that quality control is its main function.

It means ensuring that quality is an inevitable attribute at every stage. Inspection for faults comes last – and least.

Don Harrison, Production Quality Superintendent at the Melton Mowbray factory, argues that it is a waste to put your best effort, instruments and skill into inspecting quality at the end of manufacture. These should be part of the manufacturing process.

Responsibility for quality at Pedigree is therefore centred in the Production Department. Technicians and managers from other departments are involved – including research and process development. Their brief is not so much to eliminate faults as to look for improvements in every part of the manufacturing process.

The biggest section of the Production Quality Department is Technical Services. They make routine checks on everything from cooling water to the dimension of can seams. They test new products and processes. They identify day-to-day problems – and solve them.

Two smaller sections of PQD study manufacturing methods and quality controls over the longer term.

It's a mathematical, statistical approach, calculating weekly averages and variables, correlating data. Small changes in key figures can give advance notice of major problems in plenty of time to head them off. The system is based on the methods long practised by the parent company, Mars Ltd. The product is different but the principles of quality control are the same.

Sophisticated techniques of statistical analysis ensure that the information extracted from all the figures is itself of high quality and reliability. Too small a sample of production can give a misleading impression, too large a sample is wasteful. With years of experience,

PQD have built up a formidable expertise – monitoring every aspect of a complex operation and identifying where to put their efforts and money.

Sterilisation of cans in the factory is, of course, automatically controlled, but Technical Services do a regular double check by attaching a data unit to one of the cans, and sending it all through the process to record times, temperatures and pressures. Afterwards, the data is analysed by computer as part of a continuing process of cross-checks and investigations.

The dimensions of the seam on the ends of cans are also checked regularly by special gauges which feed the measurements into a data bank for analysis and comparison.

> *Quality control is the main task of everyone who works at Pedigree*

Samples of finished products are inspected at the end of the process, but that is regarded almost as an afterthought. More significant are the charts on the walls of the panel room where the sampling takes place. These reveal the trends in all the factors that have a bearing on quality.

In this room, there are daily meetings of people from most departments, with marketing, research and production nearly always represented. This is part of another vital aspect of quality control – communication. Facts and ideas are exchanged and discussed. Information is constantly feeding backwards and forwards to and from people for whom quality control is a constant preoccupation.

If new tests and procedures are needed, then full training is given to those who will be responsible for carrying them out. All concerned must understand not only what to do, but why and how. By these methods, quality control becomes more than a practice – it becomes a permanent attitude of mind in everyone working at Pedigree.

The same principles are extended by invincible logic to suppliers.

'We don't spend a lot of time', says Don Harrison, 'inspecting the quality of products coming from suppliers – that would be ridiculous. The cost of quality control is included in what we pay them, so we hold them responsible for their own quality'.

Vendor assurance assessments are carried out by Pedigree on new suppliers, and there is constant contact with old-established suppliers as part of the search for new levels of quality, linked to efficiency and economy.

Quality assurance is a way of life at Pedigree, for everyone. That is easily said, but how is it brought about? How are employees trained and motivated?

Well, in the first place, they don't call them employees – or workers or managers: everyone is an 'associate'. Everyone clocks on, and gets a weekly pay packet or cheque – including the Managing Director.

A feeling for quality – of decor, environment, comfort, courtesy – is evident in the clean, bright, spacious factory and offices. First names are the rule at and between all levels.

'The quality of our people is the most precious quality of all', says Don Harrison.

'Care is taken over recruiting the best to begin with, and even more effort is put into training and informing them.

'People must know what is expected of them, what their responsibilities are, where to go if they have a problem' says Don Harrison. 'We have monthly communication meetings to discuss just about everything in the business. We actually stop production to hold them – that's how important it is'.

First-line managers are expected to manage – holding meetings and discussions and presentations as seems necessary in their own areas. Responsibility is exercised at the lowest level in the system that is possible. If operators on machines can deal with faults, they are encouraged to do so. If they need to refer it to a specialist, they know whom to go to.

The customers of Pedigree Petfoods do not insist on quality assurance certificates or audits before they buy their tins of Chum, Whiskas or Kit-e-Kat, but they are none the less demanding of quality. They want to be assured of nutritional standards, they want their pet to enjoy the food, they want it to be totally reliable over a period of about 15 years – the normal lifetime of an animal. These are requirements that are more exacting than those for baby foods – or possibly any other canned commodity.

Pedigree guarantees that you can feed your pet on its foods exclusively, without incurring any nutritional deficiency; it guarantees they will be packed and presented properly; it guarantees they will be fair value for money.

The final arbiters, of course, are the cats and dogs themselves. They obviously like the stuff. Chum is the leading brand of dog food, and Whiskas is the biggest-selling single brand in the grocery business in Britain. The factory at Melton Mowbray is the largest cannery in Western Europe, employing 2,000 people. Pedigree must be getting something right.

Appendix 9.2   *Jaguar Cars*

> *'Our cars had luxury, style, performance – and poor quality!'*
> *'There is no middle ground for Jaguar. We are either among the best in the world – or we just can't exist'.*
> John L Egan
> Chairman
> Jaguar Cars

Sometimes a Jaguar arrives at the final vetting point with the label on the indicator stalk scratched. The workers there used to have a simple choice: dismantle the steering column and fit a new indicator stalk – or peel the label off a new stalk from stores and stick it on.

The first remedy involved time, labour and the cost of a new stalk (totally £10 to £15); the second meant rendering the cannibalised stalk unusable (cost £9).

The Quality Circle suggested that component manufacturers provide a supply of spare stick-on labels.

Problem solved: cost – pennies.

There was never anything much wrong with the design or engineering of Jaguar cars. They have always had grace, space, pace – and that touch of magic that fills a man with the desire to possess.

So why did Jaguar fail to steal the world market from Mercedes, and BMW? Was it price? No – Jaguars have always cost less than their rivals.

'She's a beauty, and I love her', explained one American devotee, 'but I can't afford a car that lets me down'.

Jaguar's reputation for unreliability was killing a car that all the world wanted to love – that, and poor productivity in the Coventry factory.

In 1979 and 1980, the recession was destroying sales in the UK, and unfavourable exchange rates were giving another twist to the downward spiral of export orders (which normally took half of Jaguar's production).

The company was heading for extinction.

In April 1980, a new Chairman came to Jaguar and marvelled at the extraordinary paradox he found. On the one hand were glowing descriptions of the new XJ6 Series III, from motoring journalists the world over.

On the other hand, John Egan found a seemingly endless catalogue of complaints from owners and dealers about failures and breakdowns.

First, he researched the facts. Hundreds of owners of Jaguars and rival cars were contacted and questioned, and their experiences correlated with warranty statistics to find how many fault codes had to be eliminated. The frightening answer was – 150.

The next move was to set up a communications system to tell everyone in the company what the problem was and how it was going to be tackled. The slogan of the campaign was 'In pursuit of perfection'.

Managers from different departments were brought together in task forces, which were allocated groups of faults to investigate and cure. The worst 12 problems were given to the board of directors.

One of the first facts to emerge was that 60% of the faults did not originate with Jaguar at all; they were in brought-in components.

John Egan went straight to the senior management of Jaguar's suppliers – and discovered that many of them were not aware of the shortcomings of their products, and were grateful to be told.

Commented one Jaguar executive: 'We had lived with some problems for so long that we had adjusted to them'.

'Adjustments' of that sort were now ruthlessly weeded out.

Jaguar insisted that all contracting firms should sign an agreement accepting responsibility for warranty costs arising from failures of their components. Jaguar also let it be known that components would be bought abroad, if foreign quality was better.

'All this seemed to concentrate the mind remarkably', says John Egan. But not all the tactics were so abrasive. At the same time suppliers were invited into the Jaguar factory – and in one extreme case a task force was actually led by a director from a component manufacturer.

Suppliers are now regarded as part of the Jaguar team, and are involved in product design at the earliest stages. Their co-operation has turned to enthusiasm.

Components are tested by the original manufacturer to Jaguar standards, and audit systems have been set up to ensure the standards are maintained.

Communicating with the workforce was a bigger and more difficult task. Many workers were bewildered and disgruntled by changes of management and policy, insecurity and frustration. If the new campaign for quality was to succeed, it had to win their hearts and minds.

The campaign began in earnest by inviting all Jaguar's dealers in the UK to the factory to talk with management and shop stewards. The talk was frank and blunt from Jaguar's side:

'Quality is a joke word on the lips of many Jaguar owners through our lack of success in achieving the standards which they and you have every right to expect. You don't need a detailed graph to know that the levels of our sales have fallen drastically, down. 50% in 1979, with these sales lost to our competitors. For every customer we lose each week, 21 jobs are put at stake.'

The speaker was Mike Beasley, Manufacturing Director. A few days later, he stopped the assembly lines, gathered the workers in the canteen and showed them a video recording of the whole conference. This was followed by a briefing session for management, supervisors and shop floor, with questions and answers all in the same down-to-earth vein.

'It was clear from the outset', says John Egan, 'that emphasising quality met with their full approval. They all wanted to win.'

But there was a hard road ahead. Time-honoured practices had to be swept aside to introduce new methods of quality control, and increase productivity. Tighter disciplines were imposed, and the total workforce was to be reduced by 30% at all levels, including supervision, inspection and rectification.

At the same time, Quality Circles were introduced, making groups of workers responsible for monitoring the quality of work coming in and going out of their area.

The philosophy had changed from one of inspecting out faults to one of building in quality.

'The consequences of this programme were quite dramatic', says John

Egan. 'We believe that the 50% sales growth we achieved in the US during 1981 was directly attributable to improved quality. We now have over 60 Quality Circles, involving 10% of our workforce. We would like to have more but we are having to reorganise our management structure to cope with the enormous enthusiasm and request for change required from these active trouble-shooting groups.'

The 'right-first-time' approach has made everything more predictable. In 1981 and 1982, model launches and production of new models began on time: 95% of total production is now on time.

In 1980, 10,500 workers made 14,105 cars.

In 1982, 7,400 workers made 22,046 cars.

In 1980, the average was 1.34 cars per man; in 1982 this had more than doubled to three cars per man.

Many of the emergency measures of 1980 have now been absorbed into regular custom and practice. Jaguar now telephones directly 150 new owners in Britain and the United States, one month after purchase, and again nine months after. That feedback is passed on to the shop floor by regular video reports on Jaguar's progress.

A note of optimism is now softening the hard-hitting style of those reports. American dealers came to visit the plant, and were interviewed.

Said one: 'We have noticed a tremendous improvement in the quality of the vehicles we have received'.

Said another: 'We can light the wick on the rocket now, and Jaguar can do more business in the States than ever in their whole history'.

The figures for 1982 proved him right. Sales in the USA were up 120%, and in the UK Jaguar sold more cars than the combined total of all its competitors in the luxury saloon sector. From 1982 to the end of the 1980s the company has wrestled with another problem: it cannot make enough cars to satisfy the demand.

Appendix 9.3   *Greendale Electronics*

> *'We have deliberately gone into high-technology areas, because they are not so price-sensitive. We are not competing with Malaysia and Taiwan.'*
> Colin Wemyss
> Managing Director
> Greendale Electronics, Sheffield

Like all firms with a quality assurance system, Greendale Electronics looks hard at the quality systems of its suppliers; and it is choosy about its customers' quality too – even if it means declining to supply them.

In today's world, that is not an easy rule to apply. The reason for it is that Greendale does not make a complete end product, like a car or a television set; its products are components for other people's machines and systems, in telecommunications, power supplies, computer terminals and vehicle test instruments. It would be bad for Greendale's reputation to be associated with a poor quality end product and it would be even worse if the company had to conform to poor design and specifications, forced on it by a customer with third-rate standards.

How does Managing Director Colin Wemyss handle these difficult and sometimes embarrassing situations?

'With difficulty', he grins, but the fact is that his company can now afford to take that sort of attitude when necessary – indeed, it can't afford not to. It is now planning to manufacture electronic components for medical instruments, where the safe margin of error is nil, and he does not believe that you can run a factory to varying standards of quality.

The kind of competition that gets the rough edge of Colin Wemyss's Scots tongue are the electronic companies that have mushroomed in recent years, and have often taken Government money without having any solid expertise behind their wares. 'We have been asked to make components to faulty designs and poor specifications, and we have had to refuse to do it', he says.

What makes him even angrier are customers who take his designs and hand them over to be made on the cheap by just such companies. 'In the end, there is only one answer', he says, 'and that is quality. That is where we defeat them.'

The success of Greendale's quality policy speaks for itself. When Crystalate Holdings, the parent company, bought Greendale five years ago, the net assets of the company were £23,000: today, they are £538,000. Crystalate's shares have gone from 5p to £1.65 over the same period.

Before the take-over, Greendale was a medium-to-low technology company making equipment mainly for the Post Office. A downturn in orders had reduced it to making camp stools, just to keep the employees in work.

Crystalate bought the company for the sake of the undeveloped skills within it, and as a vehicle for its ambitions in the electronics field.

The policy was to sell into the high-added-value, high-technology markets, and to phase out low-profit, high-volume products. A massive investment plan of half a million pounds was started. BS 9000 approval was obtained for telecommunication products for British Telecom, with a quality management system to BS 5750.

On these standards and their application, Colin Wemyss is quite inflexible, but the rest of his management style is relaxed and open. He believes that his management committee should run the company day to day, and that everyone should be free to question working practices. He sees no virtue in hierarchies or deference.

A monthly works council is the principal means of communication with the workforce, with day-to-day news passed on by supervisors.

'If we are losing money one month', he says, 'we tell them, if we have a success we make sure they know'.

But he admits that management–worker relations have not yet progressed as far as he would like. As a Scot, accustomed to working in the past with American multinationals, often with entirely new factories in new industries, he has always been used to an egalitarian, collaborative relationship from shop floor to board room. The dour scepticism of South Yorkshire came as a toe-stubbing surprise.

Traceability of worker as well as of materials, for example, is an essential part of a quality assurance system, but he encountered resistance from the operatives because they saw it as a threat. Colin Wemyss wants them to see it as a way of identifying problems of technique, so that help and training can be given where they are needed.

He recognises that many of the reactions are born of historic experience in older industries, with authoritarian management, and that human attitudes cannot be changed overnight.

He believes that bonus and productivity schemes, share options and constant communication will win hearts and minds. Already, there are signs of change. A scheme for self-certification in illness was introduced, and was followed by a marked fall in absenteeism. Two Quality Circles have been started, and are beginning to discover for themselves their own scope and purpose.

So far, quality assurance systems at Greendale have reduced the proportion of rejects (which are largely worthless in electronics) from 28% to 4%.

With 100,000 units of production a year, at an average cost of £10.80 per unit, it adds up to a saving of around a quarter of a million pounds. That figure feeds through almost entirely into profits.

One of the Quality Circles is on the production line making VDU terminals for IBM, a company that can be unforgiving of repeated quality faults, but keenly appreciative of quality improvement. Colin Wemyss and Greendale are proud to have IBM's seal of approval.

They are even prouder of the accolade they received this year – Greendale are to make a unit for a major electronics manufacturer which will go directly to its customers, without inspection by the firm concerned.

That is the meaning of quality assurance.

10 · Dunlop Holdings: Takeover

Rod Apps and Martin Reynolds

This case is concerned with the events surrounding the takeover of Dunlop by BTR. The case outlines the strategic position of Dunlop at the time Sir Michael Edwardes became Chairman and provides the background to the proposed capital reconstruction. In addition, the case provides the opportunity to apply your knowledge of the takeover process and to experience the problems associated with corporate valuation.

The downfall of Dunlop

Dunlop is usually credited with the invention of the pneumatic tyre, and it is certainly the case that the growth of the Dunlop company was based on the manufacture of tyres. In 1969, Dunlop's share of the UK tyre market was 40%: however, by 1985, Dunlop's involvement in tyre production was virtually zero.

The major changes in the tyre market originated with the development, by Michelin of France, of the 'radial' tyre. The tyres of the post-war front-wheel-drive Citroen cars gave little wear, and because of this Michelin came up with the idea of placing a steel 'brace' or 'girdle' underneath the tread of the tyre to hold the tread in place. This development not only gave dramatically improved mileage, but also provided greater strength, which resulted in the rapid adoption of the radial tyre by the truck market.

By 1985, Michelin's radial tyre had been matched – or improved upon – by all major tyre manufacturers. Pirelli developed the use of a textile girdle (the technology subsequently adopted by Dunlop), which gave superior adhesion properties, particularly in wet conditions, though at the expense of some reduction in mileage as compared with the steel-braced tyres. Dunlop was effectively the second manufacturer in the radial tyre market but found that the UK vehicle industry was, in general, slow to adopt the radial tyre: given the tendency for car owners to fit the same tyre as replacements, both the original equipment and replacement markets in radial tyres grew slowly. Dunlop did not cease its UK production of cross-ply tyres until 1981.

Sir Campbell Fraser, the Chairman of Dunlop from 1978 to 1983, is quoted as saying that, 'The tyre business is . . . in the unusual position of suffering from excellence. The steel radial tyre lasts three times as long as a conventional tyre. To last three times as long is to reduce capacity by two-thirds'. Despite these improvements in mileage to be obtained from the use of radial tyres, the majority of the European tyre manufacturers continued to prosper during the 1960s and into the 1970s, since the number of cars on the roads, and mileages driven, continued to rise. Indeed, in that period, the market grew by about 6% per annum. It did not last. The oil price rises of 1973–4 and 1979–80, the recession in 1980 and an increasing volume of imports into the European market saw the emergence of a substantial over-capacity in the industry. Dunlop's position within the industry was made worse by the halving of UK vehicle production over the course of the 1970s, and with increasing emphasis on economy in the post-oil crisis era, found itself with the wrong technology (ie textile rather than steel-braced).

In 1970, Dunlop formed a link with Pirelli of Italy and Switzerland. This was intended as a symmetrical union, where the expected advantages were seen to be a diversification of products and of markets for both Pirelli and Dunlop, and a sharing of development costs to ease the pressure on investment funds. In this way, it was hoped that Dunlop–Pirelli would be in a stronger position to compete with Michelin.

The Dunlop–Pirelli link did not succeed. Soon after its formation in 1970, Dunlop was forced to make a provision of £41.4m due to losses sustained in Italy. As continued losses by Pirelli would have destroyed the symmetry of the union, accordingly, Dunlop refused to invest in Pirelli's activities until it returned to profitability; as a consequence, Dunlop's stake in Pirelli diminished to 19% by 1981. In that year, the Dunlop management conceded that the union was not going to succeed. The Italians were ready to agree on this, since Dunlop had by then slipped into the red, and Dunlop emerged with a payment of just over £20m as recompense for 'adverse cash flow' in earlier years. The view of many commentators was that the union was excellent in principle but, as it was carried out at the wrong time, it was doomed to fail. After the split in 1981, Dunlop found itself with some advantages: in the words of Colin Hope (at the time, responsible for the European tyre business), 'It has stopped management making decisions which are half sub-standard' (since management had been worrying about the implications of any decision or development not only for Pirelli but Dunlop as well). It was further claimed that a whole layer of decision-making was removed, and managers were able to devote their time and energy to Dunlop's business.

The restructuring of Dunlop

By 1981, as Dunlop was incurring losses, there was a need for its management to sort out its tyre business. The strategy chosen was to cut out the frills and to concentrate on the high-volume products, ie, radial car and truck tyres, and motorcycle tyres. However, this was not sufficient; the European tyre business continued to make heavy losses which threatened to bring down the profitable areas of Dunlop's business. In mid-1982 the decision was taken to dispose of the European tyre business, either by closing it down (at an enormous cost in redundancies) or by selling the business. The difficulty with the latter option lay in finding a buyer for a loss-making tyre business in Europe at that time.

Dunlop approached the Japanese, not least because it was a substantial shareholder in the Sumitomo Rubber Company. In 1983 agreement was finally reached, Dunlop would sell its Sumitomo shares in Japan and Sumitomo would buy Dunlop's European tyre operations.

Dunlop had a substantial element of non-tyre business for a large part of its history, and although a lot of this business was based on rubber, an increasing proportion was not. The company had a long-standing strategy of reducing its dependence on the European tyre manufacturing business: this was reflected in its acquisition of the Angus group of diverse businesses in 1968. Throughout the period of union with Pirelli, Dunlop retained its central objectives; these were a reduction in dependence on tyres, diversification of overseas operations, and a movement towards higher technology products. The objective of diversifying its overseas operations received a setback in 1982 when Dunlop sold its Malaysian interests. This sale was against the background of increasing Malaysian nationalism, giving rise to a sensitive political situation, and to the possibility of a takeover bid for the whole Dunlop group from a Malaysian consortium. The £73m deal, though making a welcome dent in its borrowings, was not sufficient to end its financial difficulties. Dunlop's net borrowings at the end of 1981 stood at almost £350m, and were to rise to over £400m in 1983.

The extent of Dunlop's activities outside the tyre industry in earlier periods is worth noting. Even in 1970, when Dunlop's tyre business was comparatively buoyant, it only accounted for 62% of turnover and 70% of profit for the group as a whole. Four main areas of non-tyre business may be identified.

1 *Sports* In the 1970s and early 1980s, Dunlop was the largest and most broadly-based UK manufacturer of sports equipment. The two main – and competing – brands used by Dunlop were Dunlop Sports and Slazenger. This area had not been as profitable as might be expected; in recent years sport has attracted greatly increased attention but the number of participants – and therefore the volume of equipment – is not vastly different. The recession of the early 1980s, the heavy cost of sponsorship, the entry of foreign (especially American) companies into the market at the top end, and low-cost imports competing at the lower end, all combined to make this area a highly

competitive business. With increasingly sophisticated technology and materials used in many sports products, a high level of investment was necessary for long-term survival. Approximate turnover, 1984: £130m.

2   *Industrial*   This area covers the traditional end of the rubber products industry by including conveyor belting, hosing of all types for industrial machinery (including that for the off-shore oil industry) and for domestic appliances, and fluid seals for use in vehicle engines and components. It also includes higher technology precision equipment, such as seals and valves for use in the NASA space shuttle, and the application of carbon-fibre technology in medical science. Approximate turnover, 1984: £150m.

3   *Engineering*   A mainstay of this area for many years was the manufacture of automotive wheels, but it also includes complete aviation braking systems (eg for Concorde, the Harrier, and the Boeing 757) and other high-technology products, much of it emphasising the use of carbon-fibre. Approximate turnover, 1984: £100m.

4   *Consumer products*   Comprising principally of the Dunlopillo range of beds, mattresses and pillows, for which the continental and Far East markets are particularly lucrative, this area also included items such as carpets and adhesives. Approximate turnover, 1984: £100m.

After the sale of its European tyre business to Sumitomo, Dunlop's other interests at the end of 1984 comprised:

(a)   Dunlop Tire and Rubber Corporation, a specialist tyre manufacturer operating in the US in a restricted range of market niches, notably motorcycle tyres.

(b)   Dunlop South Africa, 51% owned by Dunlop, manufacturing tyres and other rubber-based equipment, and sports equipment.

(c)   Dunlop Overseas, comprising a varied range of manufacturing and trading companies in Africa, the Far East, South America and the Caribbean.

Approximate turnover of these overseas interests, 1984: £500m.

Although Dunlop achieved some small profits overall in 1983, it still had crippling debts of around £400m. Many of the 53 banks supporting this debt started to put pressure on Dunlop for changes to be made, principally to senior management. The banks insisted that Sir Michael Edwardes become Chairman of the group: Edwardes, in his turn, insisted on complete freedom of action if he moved in, and particularly as regards the removal of virtually all of Dunlop's executive board.

The appointment of Sir Michael Edwardes as Dunlop's Chairman

Sir Michael Edwardes is credited with a string of public and corporate achievements including having been Chairman of British Leyland, Chloride, Mercury Communications and ICL. His chairmanship of BL brought him public recognition and the admiration of other industrial managers; in a period when BL was plagued by industrial strife and a falling market share, he headed the team responsible for major changes in industrial relations and in revamping the company's products and image. After leaving BL, he joined Mercury Communications (part of Cable and Wireless) for a short period until joining ICL. This post was also to be short-lived as ICL was taken over by Standard Telephones and Cables in August 1984.

The arrival of Sir Michael Edwardes as executive Chairman of Dunlop Holdings in November 1984 provided the signal to the company's shareholders that the capital reconstruction – which most people outside the company had seen as inevitable a number of years before Sir Michael joined – was now only months away. Sir Michael joined Dunlop, together with two other new directors from ICL, Robin Biggam and Roger Holmes, on the understanding that a financial reconstruction of the company would come into effect. In fact, Edwardes' three-year appointment, made after lengthy negotiations and for a controversial salary, was to last for less than six months. Early in March 1985, Dunlop was taken over by BTR, a major British conglomerate, after a seven-week takeover battle.

Edwardes' immediate concern was to improve employee and shareholder morale and to convince the City that Dunlop had the necessary management and financial strength, in addition to the products and marketing skills required, to restore the company to long-term profitability and growth. The share price of Dunlop had fallen from around 260p in the late 1960s to a low of 25p in December 1984. As net asset values were eroded and dividends disappeared, the company's shareholders had seen the value of their investment dwindle. Dunlop's employees too had felt the impact in the decline of the company's fortunes; Dunlop – a company conspicuously overmanned – had shed over 50,000 jobs as a result of rationalisation, although at the end of 1984 it was still employing more than 27,000 people.

The structure of share ownership in Dunlop was unusual. The company had very few institutional investors with individual holdings measured in hundreds rather than millions. For example, at the end of 1984, Dunlop's share register consisted of some 42,000 ordinary shareholders, of whom some 80% owned 1,000 shares or less. Moreover, the typical small shareholding of the British investor was not usually acquired for either income or growth, but was often inherited, received as a birthday present or bought out of affection for an old employer. About half of Dunlop's equity was in the hands of these (mostly small) British investors, with some 25% held by American investors in American Depository Share form. However, the major single shareholding was that of Pegi Malaysia, a Malaysian investment company that owned about 25% of the equity. In theory, shareholders can influence company affairs, though the practical problems and costs of organising and communicating shareholder opinion are usually prohibitive. Representing the interests of small shareholders in Dunlop was the Dunlop Shareholders Association whose spokesman, Professor Richard Pritchard of Leicester University, feared that any capital reorganisation would totally wipe out the investment of existing ordinary shareholders.

The capital reconstruction of Dunlop

In a letter to Dunlop shareholders on 17 December 1984, the new Chairman explained that dealing in the company's shares had been temporarily suspended pending the arrangements for the financial reconstruction. At a suspended share price of 25p, the market value of Dunlop was £36m, one-third of its 1981 market value. Sir Michael Edwardes also indicated that a radically new approach to the management of Dunlop was to be implemented. The organisation was to be structured around seven profit centres: four product profit centres and three geographically-based profit centres. This structure was designed to impose greater responsibility upon new management for the investment and marketing effort associated with a particular product.

Dunlop's bankers led by Barclays, Midland and National Westminster (who jointly owned 25% of Dunlop's £425m debt), were the company's principal creditors and inevitably the financial reconstruction was going to involve a direct shareholding by the banks on a scale not normally seen in Britain. The rescue package announced in mid-January 1985 was one of the most complex financial packages put together in the history of the City. Designed to raise a total of £142m through the issue of new share capital, the amount of new equity required was beyond the capacity of existing ordinary shareholders. The support of the company's bankers and a larger number of new financial institutions was central to the plan and inevitably involved a substantial dilution in the equity holdings of existing shareholders. An extraordinary meeting of the company's shareholders was fixed for 8 February 1985, since the implementation of the capital reconstruction required the support of 75% of Dunlop's existing shareholders.

Prior to the announcement of the capital reconstruction package, the Dunlop Shareholders' Association expressed concern at the management's plan to present a non-negotiable rescue plan at an extraordinary shareholder meeting. Professor Richard Pritchard warned that if the proposals were 'grossly inequitable to the existing owners of the company

. . . we shall muster as much support as we can and will have no hesitation in voting against them'. The shareholders' association was worried that the company's new directors appeared to be more concerned with being accountable to the company's bankers than to its shareholders. The tone of the document sent to shareholders on 15 January 1985 reflected the dilemma that was facing the Dunlop board. The issue of new share capital required to make a significant reduction in the company's £535m indebtedness – and also to ensure that the principal banks maintained their existing banking facilities – required a significant write-down of the company's equity. The details of the rescue package were:

- the issue of some 800 million new ordinary shares (against some 144 million existing shares) at 14p per share. In addition, £40m worth of redeemable preference shares of £1 each at par would be issued;

- a total of £43m of ordinary shares to be offered as a rights issue to the company's existing shareholders on the basis of 15 ordinary shares for every 7 already held. A further £29m of ordinary shares were to be placed with new institutional investors;

- the conversion of £70m of bank debt into share capital by a combination of £40m worth of ordinary shares and £30m worth of redeemable preference shares;

- £170m of funds to be injected via previously announced divestments;

- the provision by the company's banks of revised borrowing facilities amounting to £260m and a reduction in capital to facilitate the payment of dividends in future years.

Despite the financial reconstruction, Dunlop Holdings' gearing – net borrowings in relation to shareholders' funds – would still remain very high. The finance director, Robin Biggam, said the gearing ratio 'would not be far removed from 1:1 by the end of 1984'. Shareholders' funds, well under £100m at the end of 1984, were expected to rise to about £200m by the end of 1985.

City fund managers gave a favourable reception to the proposals, and the re-listing of the company's shares, after an absence of six weeks from the market, reflected this. The share price rose from 25p to 31p on the first day of re-trading. But it is a debatable point whether this share price movement reflected the hopes of small investors in Sir Michael Edwardes' ability to turn Dunlop around, or whether it was the result of more fundamental financial factors.

The BTR takeover bid

As Dunlop struggled to negotiate the complex restructuring package with its banks and financial institutions in the City, BTR, under the leadership of Sir Owen Green, was monitoring Dunlop's progress with interest. BTR – which started life as the British Tyre and Rubber Company – had been closely watching Dunlop for some five years, and when in 1983 Dunlop sold its troubled European tyre business to Sumitomo of Japan, BTR started seriously to consider Dunlop as a target for a takeover.

BTR made its move two days after the 70-page document outlining the financial reconstruction had been sent to Dunlop shareholders. A 'dawn raid' early on 17 January 1985 netted BTR – for a modest investment of about £3m – some 28% of Dunlop Holdings' existing preference shares. The preference shares languishing in the market at 33p were bid for at 75p by BTR and a number of large institutional investors took advantage of this offer and provided some four million shares in a short space of time. The significance of the purchase was that it would enable BTR to block the proposed financial reconstruction of Dunlop – as Sir Owen Green stated – 'the only way to make sure we could get a bid that would run was to command the restructuring situation'.

In the space of 20 years, BTR, a highly diversified conglomerate, had grown from an obscure rubber products company, into a group with sales in excess of £3bn and pre-tax profits of about £270m at the end of 1984. BTR, and in particular its Chairman, Sir Owen Green, had established a reputation in the City of management excellence, which few, if any, could equal. The single-minded management philosophy of BTR is summarised in an oft-repeated slogan: 'Growth is the goal, profit is the measure, security is the result'. Sir Owen Green, who joined BTR in 1958 as an accountant, epitomises a strong management team in a company that pays ruthless attention to the bottom line. BTR has a remarkable history of earnings and dividend growth and a proven record of turning flagging companies into healthy profit-making organisations. A recent example of this was the acquisition of Thomas Tilling in 1983 for £670m. BTR disposed of all but one member of the Tilling's board and installed stringent financial control systems that allowed the new management team to record a 'substantial improvement' in just over a year.

After bidding for Dunlop, Sir Owen Green commented that, 'We believe that over the years, Dunlop lacked some sense of purpose and attention to the bottom line. It may be that they were prisoners of their pasts'. This comment was indicative of a 'phoney war' in which polite sparring between the BTR and Dunlop management teams emphasised the similarity between them rather than any difference in the approach that either would take in solving Dunlop's problems. Sir Michael Edwardes – being careful not to criticise Sir Owen and his team – emphasised the reason why Dunlop should retain its independence when he commented, 'Our broad approach is likely to be similar to BTR's. The difference is that Dunlop would become part of a very large conglomerate which has just digested Tilling'. The tone of the exchange of views between the BTR and Dunlop management was to change markedly in the following weeks as the takeover battle developed into a bitter dispute over management control. Both sides questioned each other's tactics and the Takeover Panel intervened to prevent the use of misleading and distorted information in influencing Dunlop's shareholders.

The terms of the initial bid for Dunlop valued the company at around £33m and was described in a press release by the Dunlop management as, 'grossly inadequate and opportunistic and should be vigorously rejected . . . After a period of uncertainty Dunlop now have a stable leadership and the prospect of achieving financial stability'. BTR's remarkable record of growth (it was trading on a p/e ratio of 27) required that it absorb and recycle major companies at regular intervals in order to maintain its record and momentum. Dunlop, with a sales turnover of just over £1bn, substantial tax losses and facing a recovery situation was an ideal acquisition for BTR.

BTR offered two new ordinary shares for every 59 Dunlop ordinary shares (valuing each Dunlop share at just over 23p) or an alternative cash offer of 20p for each Dunlop ordinary share. In addition, BTR offered 7 new BTR ordinary shares for every 55 Dunlop preference shares or alternatively 75p cash for each preference share. Upon the announcement of this initial offer, Dunlop's share price increased from 31p to 36p, with BTR shares rising 69p to an all-time high of 686p.

The outcome of the takeover was clearly going to be dependent upon the Dunlop bankers as well as its shareholders; even with £900m of shareholders' funds, BTR would be hard pushed to buy a company with over £400m debts and very little equity. Delicate negotiations between BTR and Dunlop's bankers were going to be necessary to ensure that the banks would continue to finance the company if BTR acquired control.

The Dunlop board focused its defence plan around a modified capital reconstruction package which would be more appealing to the company's shareholders. Inevitably, this was going to require that shareholders be given an opportunity to provide either all, or the bulk of, the new equity that Dunlop was planning to raise. This would enable the Dunlop management to avoid the contentious issue of a massive dilution of shareholders' equity which was implicit in the original reconstruction package. Ironically, in defending the 'new Dunlop' against the BTR bid, Sir Michael Edwardes would need to backtrack on earlier arguments and persuade shareholders that they could 'forget' the grim figures and dire health warnings which were made so explicit in the January reconstruction document.

In a letter to Dunlop shareholders in late January, Sir Michael Edwardes informed the company's shareholders that the 'offer price is lower than any price at which Dunlop's ordinary shares have been quoted on the stock market for at least 10 years' and that the bid would have to be 'massively' increased to stand any chance. This letter highlights a contentious issue in most takeover bids – namely, what value to place on a target company's shares.

BTR's initial offer of 20p and 23p for Dunlop's ordinary shares contrasted favourably with the 14p price per ordinary share that the Dunlop board proposed in the capital reconstruction package. Dunlop management argued that the market value of Dunlop's shares reflected the 'true worth' of the business and as the share price edged towards 50p on the market it became clear that BTR would need to make an improved offer if it was to win control.

As BTR's initial offer closed towards the end of February, less than 1% of the ordinary shareholders in Dunlop accepted the terms. Speculation in the City mounted as to the terms of BTR's second offer. A firm of stockbrokers, Laurie Millbank, suggested that Dunlop was probably worth at least £100m and Dunlop's financial advisers were even suggesting that a price of 100p per share would not be unreasonable; another stockbroking firm, Sheppards and Chase, suggested a net asset value of 52p per share. This diversity of opinion was not surprising, given the limited information available to Dunlop shareholders and the market about the company's performance during 1984. More significantly, where had all this extra value come from? In late December 1984, Dunlop was technically bankrupt and it was only after considerable persuasion that the banks and institutions agreed to bail Dunlop out at a price of 14p per new ordinary share. Indeed, discussion of a financial reconstruction package at the end of 1983 had suggested the issue of new shares for just 7p each!

Appendix 10.1 *Dunlop Share Price 1977–85*

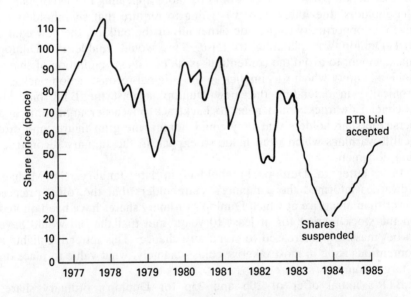

Appendix 10.2   *Summary of Results for Dunlop Group for 1980–82 (Historical Cost)*

	£m 1983	£m 1982	£m 1981	£m 1980
Turnover	1,604	1,525	1,456	1,386
Operating profit	63	41	52	50
Profit/loss before tax	17	(7)	–	10
Profit/loss attributable to Dunlop shareholders (before extraordinary items)	(28)	(52)	(41)	(15)
Earnings per share (before extraordinary items)	(20.4p)	(36.7p)	(29.4p)	(11.3p)
Dividends per ordinary share	–	2.0p	4.0p	4.0p
Capital employed at 31 December	252	379	341	416
Debt/equity ratio	130%	93%	93%	69%
Total assets less current liabilities	352	695	640	719

Appendix 10.3   *Dunlop Group Balance Sheet 1983*

	1983 £m
Fixed assets	
Tangible assets	355
Investments	37
	392
Current assets	
Stocks	333
Debtors	318
Deferred proceeds from divestment	4
Assets under contract for sale	–
Investments	2
Cash at bank and in hand	83
	740
Creditors: amounts falling due within one year	
Short-term borrowings	425
Other creditors	355
	780
Net current (liabilities)	
Total assets *less* current liabilities	352
Creditors: amounts falling due after more than one year	
Debentures and loans	61
Other creditors	25
	86
Provisions for liabilities and charges	43
	223
Capital and reserves	
Called up share capital	87
Share premium account	48
Revaluation reserve	100
Profit and loss account	(110)
	125
Minority shareholders' interests	98
	223

Appendix 10.4(a)

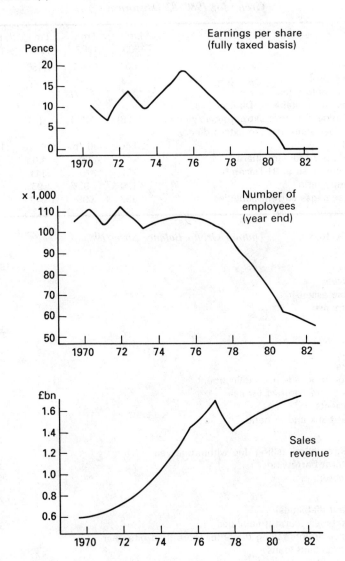

Appendix 10.4(b)

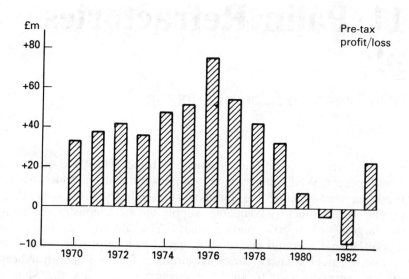

Appendix 10.4(c)

World Tyre Market, 1983

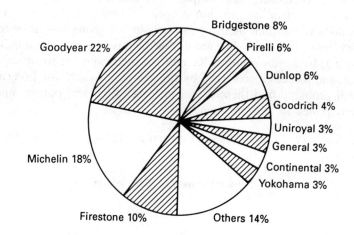

Total sales value: £27 b

11·Palin Refractories plc

Glyn Owen and John Patterson

Palin Refractories plc produces magnesia bricks which are used to line steel furnaces. Whilst the company supplies refractory products for other users, eg glass-making, the *Tribnian* steel industry takes over 75% of output. Four refractory companies supply the steel industry and Palin is the largest with a 50% market share. You are the newly appointed marketing manager and one of your first tasks is to produce a hard forecast of the steel industry's brick requirement for 1988 and an indicative medium term forecast to 1992. In giving you this task the Managing Director made the following comments:

'Of course we are extremely reliant on the steel industry, so you will need to begin by forecasting steel output. Demand for steel depends heavily on general industrial output, but it seems to me that the steel industry always does worse than industry as a whole – it grows less in boom and contracts more in slumps. We are not in the business of general industrial forecasting, because we simply haven't got the resources, so we subscribe to economic forecasts produced by the Sunbury Centre for Forecasting. You will probably find these useful in forecasting steel output, and it is company policy to rely on them.'

The Sunbury Centre has just provided Palin's with the following forecasts:

Year	Forecast growth in manufactured output
1988	+2.0%
1989	+2.4%
1990	+3.5%
1991	−0.5%
1992	+1.5%

As part of your investigations you discuss the technology of steel-making with Palin's Technical Director, and he concludes by saying:

'Yes, we do rely heavily on the steel industry, but it is not as simple as that. There are three main steel-making processes, and each uses different amounts of brick. In 1987 usage was:

Process		Mag brick usage/tonne of steel Kg
Basic Open Hearth	(BOH)	20.5
Basic Oxygen	(BO)	5.6
Electric Arc	(EA)	3.8

'It's a great pity for us that the basic open hearth (BOH) process is obsolete and is being phased out. BOH production will probably fall by 30% during 1988 and a further 30% in 1989 – I doubt that it will be used at all in the 1990s. The other two processes should continue to be used in the same proportions as in 1987, but technical progress is steadily increasing furnace efficiency in the big oxygen converters and brick usage will decline by about 5% per annum for the foreseeable future.'

From official statistics you find that BOH, BO, and EA processes accounted respectively for 9%, 53%, and 38% of steel production in 1987. You have also found industrial production figures and steel production figures for the Tribnian economy for the years 1968 to 1987; these are given in the table below:

Year	Index of manufactured output 1980 = 100	Steel production (million tonnes)
1968	98.9	29.0
1969	102.6	30.0
1970	103	30.6
1971	102.3	27.6
1972	105.1	28.3
1973	113.8	30.8
1974	108.7	28.6
1975	105	25.2
1976	106.5	25.9
1977	108.2	25.6
1978	109	25.6
1979	109.4	26.8
1980	100	18.6
1981	94	15.2
1982	94.2	13.7
1983	96.9	15.0
1984	100.7	15.2
1985	103.8	15.7
1986	104.5	15.1
1987	110.5	18.2

Further research reveals that in 1980 there was a long-lasting (three months) steelworkers' strike as a protest against the Tribnian government's proposed steel-plant closure policy. The strike failed and closures quickly reduced overall capacity from about 30m tonnes pa to 18m tonnes pa.

12 · Dronfield Tool & Instrument Company

John Patterson and Maurice Brown

The Dronfield Tool & Instrument Company, a closely held private firm, was established in 1946 by David Cole, a trained engineer, after his demob from the RAF. The company specialises in high-quality hand tools and a range of close tolerance measuring instruments used in the engineering industries. The business grew steadily, if unspectacularly, over the next 35 years until in 1985 the founder died after a long illness.

The major shareholder in the firm is David Cole's widow, with a minority of shares held by other close relatives. On the instructions of Mrs Cole the company has been managed since 1985 by Max Gray, the long-serving Company Secretary, and equally long-standing family friend. It is well known by the employees that the remaining family has no interest in the firm beyond drawing a steady income in annual dividends. David Cole, a strong personality, had never tolerated interference in the way he ran the company and had clear ideas as to how he wanted it to develop. Despite his authoritarian style of management, he was greatly respected by the shopfloor workers, most of whom are time-served, highly skilled craftsmen, with long service at Dronfield's. They felt that his decisions, though sometimes hard, were fair and they respected his judgement and engineering ability.

Contact between David Cole and his management had been personal and direct, and management meetings were rare and always on an *ad hoc* basis. Cole was usually prepared to listen to the expert advice given by his management, although he was prone to ignore it if it did not support his views.

Max Gray attempted to continue the management style of his predecessor, and if anything, took an even harder line at shopfloor level. This has caused a great deal of resentment and there had been several unofficial stoppages, which, whilst not of a serious nature, are generally regarded as being symptomatic of an overall dissatisfaction and loss of motivation.

Whilst Gray has formalised the contact with his management by instituting regular meetings, these have tended to become more order-giving sessions with little real communication. The relationship between Gray and Bell is tolerable probably because of their common financial background, but Gray's standing in the eyes of Grice and especially Waite and McTell is very low indeed. Gray is regarded by most of the people at

Dronfields as lacking any long-term policy and as reacting to short-term events in a distinctly *ad hoc* manner.

There is now a general feeling that the company badly lacks Cole's guiding hand, and is going downhill. Of course the firm has been affected by recession, but there is more to the malaise than that.

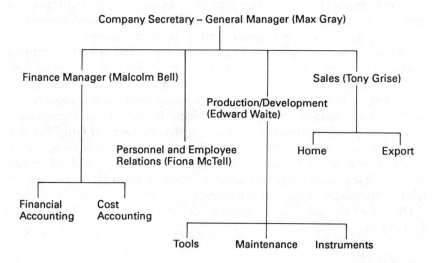

Company Secretary – General Manager (Max Gray)

Finance Manager (Malcolm Bell)   Sales (Tony Grise)

Production/Development (Edward Waite)

Personnel and Employee Relations (Fiona McTell)   Home   Export

Financial Accounting   Cost Accounting

Tools   Maintenance   Instruments

In organisation the company is operated on a functional structure, as shown in the table. Malcolm Bell, approaching retirement age, has worked for the company since 1950 and continued to exercise the Cole philosophy of tightly controlling the internal allocation of funds; this effectively meant that virtually no product development work has been done since the late 1970s.

Edward Waite, a graduate engineer in his thirties, was appointed after the founder's death in 1985 to ensure that the tradition of high quality of products continued. However, he recognised that in spite of the established name of the company the company's products, particularly on the measuring side, were technologically falling behind market leaders. He felt extremely frustrated about the meagre allocation of development funds – in spite of the bright ideas he had for introducing micro-electronic applications to measurement – and was considering moving on to greener pastures.

Tony Grice, another relatively new member, was well aware of, and in sympathy with, Waite's views. Grice knew that although the company appeared to have a strong base in small tools this section of the market was not only flat but was being eroded by Third World producers. Grice's personal view was that the firm should stop manufacturing small tools and concentrate its resources and expertise on high value-added modern measuring instruments. He suggested this to Gray and also argued that a foothold could be maintained in the home small tool market by importing sub-contracted tools from Taiwan and marketing them under the Dronfield brandname. This latter suggestion outraged both Gray and Bell, and offended the engineer Waite. Grice decided to explore the possibility of a buy-out and he approached Waite and McTell to see if they were interested in joining him and if they would help in producing a feasibility study to persuade financial institutions to provide funds. McTell in particular had a key role in assessing shopfloor attitudes to changes in working practices and manning levels which would accompany the reorganisation of the company and its product strategy.

Clearly, major changes would have to be made, and in particular there would need to be a transition from small batch manufacture using high levels of skill to more of a mass production approach with a consequent de-skilling of the task. Retraining the existing workforce is regarded as preferable to redundancy, but the problems are seen to be formidable.

A major problem would be overcoming the resistance of Gray and Bell and in deciding an offer price. The offer price would have to appeal to Mrs Cole – it was felt that the minority shareholders would follow her lead – yet be sufficiently attractive to interest financial institutions in lending the funds to the buy-out team.

Details of the company's financial records are attached (Appendices 12.1–12.5).

Appendix 12.1
Balance Sheets of Dronfield Tool & Instrument Co

Liabilities	£(000s) 1986	1987	Assets	(£000s) 1986	1987
Ordinary share capital			*Fixed assets*		
600,000 £1 ord shares	600	600	Plant, equipment and		
Revenue reserve	400	420	buildings at cost	1,630	1,800
			Less Depreciation	400	500
Net worth	1,000	1,020		1,230	1,300
Debenture stock			*Current assets*		
8% First Mortgage			Stocks	355	350
Stock	520	500	Debtors	250	300
10% Unsecured Loan			Market investments	175	130
Stock	200	200	Cash	55	20
	720	700		835	800
Current liabilities					
Creditors and accruals	100	150			
Short-term loans	110	100			
Corporation tax	135	130			
	345	380			
Total liabilities:	£2,065	£2,100	Total assets	£2,065	£2,100

Appendix 12.2

Profit and Loss Account
Dronfield Tool & Instrument Co
For the Year Ended 31 December 1987

		£'000s
Sales		3,200
Cost of goods sold		2,755
Gross profit		445
Less Operating expenses:		
Selling costs	30	
Office administration	32	
Lease payment	28	90
Gross operating income		355
Less Depreciation		100
Net operating income		255
Add Investment income		15
		270
Less Other expenses:		
Interest on short-term loan	10	
Interest on mortgage stock	40	
Interest on unsecured loan	20	70
Profit before tax:		200
Corporation tax:		80
Net profit available to ordinary shareholders		£120

Earnings per share 20 pence

Appendix 12.3

Retained Earnings Statement
For Year Ended 31 December 1987

	£'000s
Balance of retained earnings as at 31 December 1986	380
Add: Net Profit for 1987	120
	500
Less: Dividend paid to ordinary shareholders	100
Balance of retained earnings as at 31 December 1987	£400

Appendix 12.4

Comparative Performance of
Dronfield Tool & Instrument Co
to the Small Tool Industry

Current ratio:	Industry average 2.5
Quick ratio:	Industry average 1.0
Debt ratio:	Industry average 33%
Times interest earned ratio:	Industry average 8.9 times
Fixed charge cover ratio:	Industry average 5.5 times
Stock turnover ratio:	Industry average 7.0
Fixed asset turnover ratio:	Industry average 5.0 times
Total asset turnover ratio:	Industry average 2.0 times
Margin on sales:	Industry average 5.0%
Return on total assets:	Industry average 10.0%
Return to shareholders' funds:	Industry average 15.0%

Appendix 12.5

Trend in Company Performance

Sales as a % of 1966 sales:	Up to 1985 Dronfield Tools performed better than the industry average.
Current ratio:	Since 1966 Dronfield has been around the industry average; if anything better than the average.
Debt ratio:	Always higher than the industry average, but the gap has widened since 1985.
Fixed asset turnover:	Up to 1985 better than the industry average, but progressively worse since.
Return on net worth:	Up to 1985 better than the industry average, but progressively worse since.

13·Crossed wires at British Telecom

Bill Richardson

This case study is based on research including reference to media articles. It is not intended as a comment on the handling of a business situation but as an aid to class discussion of business policy issues.

'The span of our activities and services, the technology, the requirements of our customers, the increasing strength and breadth of home competition and the pattern of regulation are, as expected, all moving on' claimed BT chairman Sir George Jefferson as he announced the 1986 reorganisation of British Telecom. Telecom's UK network operation was to be regrouped into an Inland Communications division and a Business Services division. The Business Services division was to comprise of two units – one handling general business networks operations and the other handling the specialist needs of large business customers. The reorganisation also created a new International Products division. The basic organising principles of 'devolved responsibility with accountability' were to continue to underlie the new organisation structure.

One year on from the reorganisation, BT's top management could look back on a range of mixed opinions over the level of success the organisation had achieved, since its privatisation, in adapting to its business situation. Mid 1987 seemed like a particularly pertinent time to reflect on the past, look forward to the future and take stock of the present.

In fact, in the space of six turbulent years British Telecom, in a variety of legally constituted forms and under different organisational names, had experienced much change and adaptation. Some important dates and events leading to present activities towards a declared objective of 'creating an organisation that can match the best telecommunications company anywhere in the world' had included:

1979: The Government announced the reorganisation of the General Post Office through the separation of its telecommunications services from its postal and banking services.

1981: The Act of Parliament setting up the new British Telecommunications corporation received Royal Assent on 27 July and the corporation came into being on 1 October 1981.

1982: The Government announces plans to turn British Telecommunications Corporation into a public limited company.

1983: The British Telecom Unions Committee (BTUC) launches a massive campaign against privatisation alleging that the inevitable thrust for profits would dictate adverse BT policies and attitudes towards its customers and personnel. The Post Office Engineers Union (POEU) commenced a programme of industrial action.

1984: The Telecommunications Act enables British Telecom to be transformed from a public corporation into a Public Limited Company.

1985: British Telecom plc comes into being. The selling of 51% of shares realises £4bn. 80% of British Telecom staff use their own money to buy shares over and above their allocation of free shares.

1986: Competition, already active in the customer services market, is also introduced into the more lucrative telephone network market. The Government grants a licence to Mercury Communications Ltd which is owned jointly by Cable & Wireless (40%), British Petroleum (40%) and Barclays Merchant Bank (20%).

Management could also look back, in 1987, using a functional perspective, to view British Telecom's more recent, privatised, developments.

Financial performance since privatisation, for example, in terms of turnover and profits had been improving by more than 10% each year. A variety of performance and other statistics is available in Appendix 13.1 and is worth perusal at this stage.

Financial strength had enabled BT to become a huge investor in *R&D* activities. R&D expenditure, planned at £2,100m (up 35% on 1984 levels) evidenced the longer-term aspirations and plans of the BT management. The massive investment programme in this area since privatisation was a stimulator of some of the present developments being undertaken by BT in areas such as:

The network: Inland telephone call volume was growing at a rate of around 7% per annum, overseas calls at a rate of 13% per annum. In 1985, 'cellnet', BT's joint venture with Securicor had been launched. Modern digital systems were now being installed at the rate of one every working day. Recently, work had begun on a £50m optical fibre network linking BT's customers in the City of London.

New systems and services: As part of a £700m computerisation programme, the directory enquiry and customer service systems were being updated and improved.

The community: A £160m programme to modernise payphones had already provided a higher total number of payphones than had existed two years earlier, with over half having modern equipment and many taking Phonecards.

Satellite   BT had always been a world leader in satellite
communication: communications. Earth stations in Cornwall and Hert-
                         fordshire together link the UK with more than 100
                         countries. A third earth station, the London Teleport,
                         transmits six TV channels around the UK and Europe.

Sir George Jefferson told shareholders that BT's continuing strength made it possible to invest more than ever before to improve the service to customers and secure the future prosperity of the company for shareholders and staff alike.

In a *marketing* sense Telecom was now clearly perceived as a commercially orientated service. It was the UK's second largest advertiser with a promotional budget of over £40m.

'Busby', 'It's for You-Hoo' and the 'Animals' media campaigns had helped to stimulate growing numbers of telephone calls (a central objective of BT during recent years). 'Live' testing of ads – Telecom literally measured the number of calls made after each showing of the three ads – had been applauded for its ingenuity. However, the fact that figures were never divulged led to rumours that the 'It's for You-Hoo' campaign had been dropped not for its lack of success but more because Telecom didn't get on with its account team at the agency 'KMP'. Four agencies presently share the BT account – each with its own target market to appeal to (JWT – 'residential users'; Abbott and Mead – 'individual customers at work'; Bartle Bogle – 'individual customers in a management role'; Colmans – 'specialist audiences' [such as the tourist industry]).

While competition was only slowly making its presence felt in the telephone network market, more intense competition in the equipment market maintained lower levels of profitability in this sector. Nevertheless, the equipment market was viewed as a complementary and necessary adjunct to successful business in the more lucrative network segment.

Despite declared objectives of more flexible, efficient and attractive customer interactions and products/services, BT had been subjected to growing criticism over standards of customer service. Accusations of declining standard of service and higher charges – particularly in the context of domestic customers – prevailed.

In 1987, MPs referred, in the House of Commons, to BT's abuse of monopoly power and its appalling treatment of customers.

The National Consumer Council produced a 1987 report which alleged a worsening service record.

The Telecommunication Users' Association joined the criticism bandwagon claiming a marked deterioration in service – for business and domestic users alike.

Complaints were about crossed lines, high costs, crackling connections, and the length of time being taken to install new systems and/or make repairs to existing ones.

The NCC also complained that since privatisation, BT had stopped publishing its quality of service measurements because of their 'commercial sensitivity'. The TUA blamed the poor performance in part, on too few engineers.

The Office of Telecommunications (OFTEL), the Government-created consumer orientated 'watchdog' and regulator also added fuel to the argument against BT's customer service record with its 1987 report which concurred that standards seemed to be falling (48% of people wanting to use a call box had been unable to find one that was working, for example). The Director General of OFTEL, Professor Bryan Carsberg, said 'BT has insufficient incentive under the present arrangement to repair faults quickly and to accept a contract commitment for dates for providing a new service'. He threatened the introduction of a system of financial penalties against BT if its record did not improve.

In response to such criticisms, BT management steadfastly refuted them, claiming instead that:

(1)   Service had, in fact, improved since privatisation (the Chairman's 1986 speech to shareholders, for example, had referred to the 1980 list of 250,000 people hoping for the chance of a phone – with virtually no choice of equipment – and compared this to the wide choice now available and the lack of any significant waiting list).

(2)   Complaints had increased because of publicity surrounding the privatisation of BT.

(3)   Some problems were inevitable because of:

(a)   years of under investment in a nationalised industry

(b)   the need to handle an exercise equivalent, according to one BT spokesman, to changing engines on Concorde in mid-Atlantic.

BT management felt that the growing levels of competition were sufficient sources of regulation to ensure acceptable consumer responsiveness.

City analysts tended to agree with Telecom's perceptions in this area, feeling generally that what was being witnessed were the natural re-birth pangs of an industry converting itself into a commercial organisation and undergoing a technological revolution.

If consumers felt unhappy about their interactions with Telecom, *Personnel* seemed even more dissatisfied with their situation since privatisation. Clerical and engineering staff were concerned that job losses (see Appendix 13.2) would become *the* means for increasing profits. New technology seemed set to make inroads into labour-intensive areas of work such as exchange maintenance and operator services. The BT organisational objectives of efficiency through the streamlining of workforces, the introduction of more flexible working practices and the implementation of new technology was, in the eyes of many staff, translating into job insecurity and worsening job conditions. Unions accused BT management and the Government of going back on promises of 'no job losses through privatisation'. In a radio debate, Bill Chatham, for BT's management, claimed that job losses had been created only through natural wastage. Brian Kenny for the Clerical union countered that increasing workloads justified the *creation* of jobs and that as a major employer, BT had a responsibility to be a provider of jobs and not a destroyer of them.

In conversation, rank and file staff agreed that their levels of pay were comparatively high and felt that the industrial unrest within the organisation was not so much about wages but more about a reaction to a new aggressive and callous management style and a lack of recognition for the contribution they were making to the commercial success of BT. They also felt resentful of the fact that a perceived need to introduce more commercially orientated management had produced an inequitable move towards increasing the size of management at a time when the workforce was being pressed to produce more for less.

In early 1987, a 76% vote in favour of industrial action by NCU clerical group members was in direct contradiction with management claims that BT's staff had been happy with their pay and conditions since privatisation. Appendix 13.2 offers information on both sides to the dispute. In January 1987, engineers came out on strike after management had reportedly locked them out for refusing to sign pledges of normal working.

The unions' standpoint summarised by John Golding, NCU's General Secretary, had remained consistent since the news that BT was to be privatised . . . 'higher prices, new charges and lower quality of service are faults which will not be cleared until BT's top management stops putting profits first'. Neither did the unions have confidence in OFTEL as an adequate overseer/regulator of the telecommunications industry. Rather the call was for a return to public ownership with Mercury, 'the cream skimming competition' inside BT.

Three years on from privatisation, then, British Telecom's top management had many favourable results and resources to reflect on during the course of any strategic evaluation which they might have undertaken. Despite environmental problems and growing competition, a number of opportunities for further development and growth would also be apparent from such an exercise. Plainly evident, also, however, were a number of 'crossed wires' which clearly and urgently demanded application of top management's planning and decision-making skills.

Appendix 13.1(a) *Financial Performance of British Telecom*
Source: OBSERVER (Data Stream)

Financial Year Ending 31 Mar	1973	1975	1977	1979	1980	1981	1982	1983	1984	1985	1986	1987	1988*
Turnover (£m)	1,002	1,388	2,658	3,258	3,601	4,570	5,763	6,414	6,876	7,653	8,387	9,424	7,556
Pre-tax profit (£m)	N/A	N/A	N/A	N/A	317	570	936	1,031	990	1,480	1,810	2,067	1,694
Return on capital employed	N/A	N/A	N/A	N/A	N/A	N/A	N/A	19.3%	17.5%	19.1%	20.9%	21.9%	N/A
Total number of employees	N/A	N/A	N/A	N/A	N/A	N/A	253,262	245,976	241,174	238,304	233,711	236,461	N/A

* 9 months to Dec only
▶ Time of privatisation

Appendix 13.1(b) *Share Performance of British Telecom*
Source: Sunday Telegraph

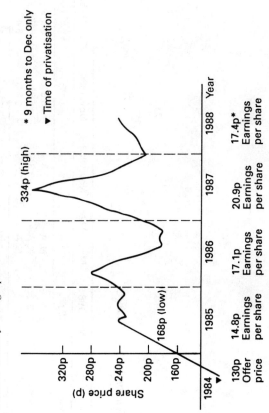

Appendix 13.1(c) *British Telecom Recorded Complaints*

Complaints	Year
10,000	1985
16,000	1986
24,000	1987

Appendix 13.1(d) *British Telecom's Price Changes*
Source: OFTEL (1987)

		Nov 1981	May 1982	Nov 1983	Nov 1984	Nov 1985	Nov 1986	Nov 1987
Rental	Line & Phone	+12.5%	N/A	+4.8%	+7.1%	+8.5%	+3.7%	0%
Local Calls	Peak	+7.5%	N/A	+2.3%	+6.8%	+6.4%	+18.9%	0%
	Standard	+115%	N/A	+2.3%	+6.8%	+6.4%	+6.4%	0%
	Cheap	+7.5%	N/A	+2.5%	+6.8%	+6.4%	-3.6%	0%
Trunk Calls	Peak	+7.5%	-33%	+2.3%	-11%	-15%	-12%	0%
	Standard	+34%	-40%	+2.6%	-5%	-20%	-12%	0%
	Cheap	+20%	-24.9%	+2.3%	+6.4%	+6%	-12%	0%

Appendix 13.1(e)   *Change Comparison*
Source: Financial Times, April 1987

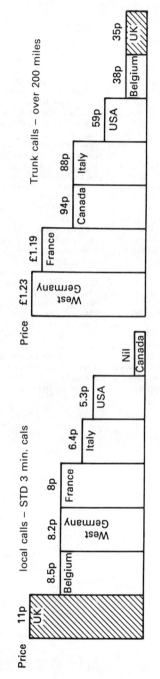

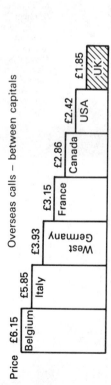

Appendix 13.2

WE'VE HAD ENOUGH!

- Pay offer rejected!
- Massive vote for industrial action!
- Members walkout in protest!

NCU clerical group members in British Telecom voted to take industrial action and rejected BT's insulting pay offer, thereby bursting the bubble of Ian Vallance's day dream assertions that BT's staff are happy with their pay and conditions of service since privatisation.

Following the ballot which resulted in 76% members voting to reject the offer, members walked out in disgust at the end of their core time, on Monday, 24th November.

Management's immediate response was to threaten suspensions and loss of pay and even the ending of flexitime until the end of the dispute.

Such was the resolve of the membership, that in the face of this provocation many members were reluctant to go back the following day.

Indeed members have been so angered by BT's intent to dock pay for the hours they were absent that many branches are taking legal advice and challenging BT's right to deduct pay for hours they were not contracted to work.

Management's tactics have been to try and instil fear in our members whilst at the same time they have attempted to persuade them that the pay offer is generous.

British Telecom are devoted to a propaganda war of truth bending.

Despite this our members are aware of the justice of their case in pursuing a wage increase that recognises the part they have played in BT's success and that does not contain strings which will worsen their conditions of service and job prospects.

The message is clear! We are sick of increasing workloads! We are sick of the use of overtime to reduce staffing levels! We are sick of the manipulation of flexitime by management. We are sick of no reward for the massive amount of profits we make each year! We want recognition by management of the successes we have made for British Telecom.

ENGINEERS   PLEDGE
SUPPORT

Dave Morris, Chairperson of the Engineering Groups Pay Committee pledged the Engineering group's support for a joint pay campaign and joint industrial action with the Clerical Group. Speaking at the Broad Strategy conference, he said, "We are not going to leave the common table bargaining that we are in. We'll be with you in two weeks time. The engineering group will be strongly supporting your executive and we are strongly committed to a common settlement!"

14 · Start-Master Ignition Systems

Peter L Jennings

Bobby Barrett had never been a brilliant speedway rider, but when it came to tuning racing machines, he was a genius! Towards the end of last season he had developed a revolutionary electronic ignition system which improved the power output of his bikes and added a late flourish to his career. At 34 his competitive racing days were over and he decided to turn his attention to marketing his electronic ignition system to speedway riders, who had once been his rivals on the track. He set up his business in the workshop attached to his home, and employed a young electronics graduate to build the ignition units. The units could be fitted without modification to any of the existing speedway machines.

Most units were sold on a 'mail order' basis and Bobby Barrett guaranteed a same day postal despatch service. Occasionally units would be delivered personally on one of Bobby's frequent visits to local speedway tracks. Whatever the means of delivery Bobby always insisted on a 'cash with order' sale, believing this to be the best method of avoiding cash flow difficulties.

Sales improved steadily during the early weeks of the new season as the Start-Master Ignition system proved to be superior to the conventional units. 140 units were sold between 1 March and 1 June. More and more orders were being taken in person at race meetings and Bobby was frequently asked if he could supply other spare parts and accessories. It soon became clear that there was the opportunity to make sales of a full range of essential items, if only the stock could be made available at the track when it was needed.

Bobby made a list of the additional items and expenses he thought he would need:

Van	£7,200	Depreciate over 5 years
Stocks	?	Variable each month
Running expenses	£200	Per month.

'I won't need any extra room. There is plenty of space in the workshop and the van can always live in the garage' thought Bobby. 'I'll have to buy the van on credit, probably a bank loan, and I don't want to borrow more than £5,000. I want to pay off the loan before the end of the season in October because sales will fall over the winter months. I'd better check my sales forecast and expenses to see if I can afford it'.

Sales Forecast – Start-Master Ignition Systems

June	July	Aug	Sept	Oct	Nov	Dec
56	60	60	56	40	20	10

Each unit sells at £75 each

Expenses

	June £	July £	Aug £	Sept £	Oct £	Nov £	Dec £
Raw materials	560	600	600	560	400	300	200
Wages	1,250	1,250	1,250	1,250	1,250	1,250	1,250
Services (Electricity)	200	220	220	200	160	150	140
Administration	100	110	110	100	80	60	50
Depreciation on equipment	100	100	100	100	100	100	100
	2,210	2,280	2,280	2,210	1,990	1,860	1,740

'Of course, if I am able to start selling other spares, I must remember to add in the extra sales and expenses,' thought Bobby. 'I'd estimate I could sell:

June	July	Aug	Sept	Oct	Nov	Dec	Jan	Feb
£2,000	£2,500	£2,500	£2,000	£1,500	£1,000	£800	£800	£1,000

'Working on 100% profit margin and assuming I can sell spares by mail order to the USA, Australia and New Zealand during our closed season, I reckon I'll need to carry two months' advance stock to cope with delivery times from the manufacturers. I want to pay for my stocks on delivery, too. It's too much trouble to keep pace with how much I would owe. Now let's see, I've got £3,000 in the bank at the moment, the loan will cost 12% pa in interest . . .'

After three hours, Bobby was still no nearer an answer. 'I think I'll have to get some help on this' said Bobby to himself. 'All I want to know is, is my business profitable, can I afford to buy the van and start selling spares and will I be able to pay off the loan by the end of October?'

Help Bobby find an answer to his questions.

15·What Next?

Bill Richardson

In the space of five short but increasingly hectic years of self-generated change, Next plc has changed the fortunes of its founding parent company and the face of British fashion retailing. A look back over its developments and some of the forces and philosophies behind them seems, inevitably, to stimulate the question 'What Next?'.

Some Organisational Developments

1981   ★ J Hepworth Ltd, the menswear manufacturer and retailer, appoints George Davies to lead the development of a chain of women's fashionwear shops.

1982   ★ With Davies as Managing Director, Next plc begins trading.

1984   ★ Next for Men chain is launched.

        ★ Hepworth computer services begin a 3-year project using IBM point of sale terminals in the Next outlets to improve and integrate purchase order management, stock distribution and replenishment, sales collation, financial planning and forecasting.

1985   ★ Next Interior launched.

        ★ Hepworth's becomes subsumed by Next.

        ★ Leeds Head Office is relocated in Leicestershire.

        ★ Total ownership is taken of Club 24 (formerly run with Forward Trust). Club 24 provides credit facilities for Next customers and for the customers of other stores such as Dixons, Mothercare and Etam.

1986   ★ Next franchises opened in Norway, Cyprus, Qatar and Antwerp.

        ★ Paul James Knitwear manufacturer is bought.

★ Grattan, the number four British mail order
organisation, is bought for £300m.

★ Next Collection, aimed more specifically at Next's
working women customers, and Next Too, directed at
existing customer bases but concentrating on more
casual garments, are launched.

1987 ★ A programme of bigger 'Complete Next', city centre
stores developments begins.

★ £338m buys Combined English Stores, the Zales to
Salisbury retailer. Next's bid is accepted in the face of
competition from Gerald Ratner of the newly successful
Ratners plc, and from Etam plc. The purchase provides
an extra 700,000 square footage of selling space
(increasing existing Next space by 80%) and takes the
pressure off Next's planned 400,000 square foot per year
growth programme.

★ Fil a Fil, a retailer of men's and women's fashions, is
bought for £800,000. Its chain of 400 ft to 500 ft retail
premises are to be used as additional outlets for Next's
shoes and accessories shops.

★ £3m is paid for a 51% interest in Van Overdijk, a
Belgian suitmaker. Next considers itself an informed
investment partner working with, rather than
controlling, the existing management.

★ Acquires 50% interest in Paige Group from Great
Universal Stores which receives £4.5m Next shares (a
1.27% stake in return). Paige offers a 197-strong chain
of womenswear shops doing little more than breaking
even.

★ Dillons, a 270 outlet chain of newsagents, is bought in
connection with Next's 'revolutionary plans for its mail
order business'. Next plans are said to include two-day
mail order responses to telephone orders and
newsagency collection points. This acquisition is greeted
with some scepticism by business commentators.

★ Sixteen Next BG stores (Boys and Girls) are opened.
Six of these are autonomous, the others forming
independent sections in Next grown up shops. Forty
such outlets are intended by the end of the year.

George Davies

Any study of this period Next quickly reveals that it is almost impossible to separate the systems, structures and strategies of the organisation from its Managing Director (and newly incumbent chairman) George Davies, with the organisation reflecting his philosophies and ideas in a wide variety of ways. Born in Liverpool in 1942, the son of a sausage and pie production manager father and a Post Office worker mother, George Davies went on to attend Bootle Grammar School and Birmingham University. He threw in his dentistry studies in 1960 after getting the bug for retailing from holiday jobs at Littlewoods. His first full-time job (with Littlewoods) was followed in 1970 by his own children's wear mail order venture (which ultimately failed). In 1974, following the demise of the business, Davies joined Pippa Dee, the party plan home sales fashion company. A successful era with this organisation ended, however, in 1981 after a boardroom row following a takeover battle. Within a matter of days, however, his contacts in the industry had put him in touch with Hepworth's, the UK's second biggest menswear manufacturer/retailer. Struggling to come to terms with a situation which had seen UK annual sales of men's suits fall during the 1970s from volumes of 10 millions to 4 millions, Hepworth, via its chairman, Terence Conran, appointed Davies. His immediate task was to take Hepworth, via women's fashion, into the new retailing era of the 1980s. His retail background provided Hepworth with, to use Davies' own words, '. . . a broadly based business guy who sees keeping in touch with the customer as vital'.

Davies is definitely a 'hands on' manager who involves himself in all areas of product market operations and in the range of functional activities. He has the capacity to take on and contribute to the range of business operations from warehousing to computer systems design and continues to take the lead in thinking up and implementing new strategic ideas. Total commitment to Next, and an obvious enjoyment of his job, sees him spending Saturday evenings at home with wife Elizabeth (production director of Next) attaining 'a big turn-on still' from checking out trading results for the week via his portable computer. Last year's Mauritius holiday produced little in the way of a suntan but more in the form of an acquired garment manufacturer. 'He spent all day, every day, in the factory', Elizabeth says. Davies kits himself out, almost entirely, in Next clothes.

Above all, perhaps Davies is an 'Ideas Man' and a quick learner. While Terence Conran reminds us that Davies was not the only person behind the Hepworth to Next transformation – 'I'm tired of hearing that George Davies reinvented the High Street. It was Conran Design Group which designed the stores and John Stephenson who now works at Storehouse who came up with the name. Now all we hear is young George getting all the credit.' Davies has, nevertheless, undoubtedly been in the driving seat for the development of the Next concept. While Davies freely admits that the original concept was not so well-formulated as it appears to have been with hindsight, he reminds us that 'we quickly realised that we had something really special going for us'. The success with which he has refined and developed the concept and associated Next operations won him the Guardian Young Businessman Award for 1985.

Colleagues refer to Davies not only as an exceptional ideas man but also one who creates the sort of atmosphere in which people want to work. Analysts regard him highly, referring to his effective management style (*everyone* calls him George), his high reputation and his ability to build a team which has, according to some commentators, 'people in the lower levels who are capable of meeting the high standards he sets'. Personnel and associates are also aware that underneath the open door management style is a tough operator capable of single-minded dogmatism over his Next ideas and plans.

Davies considers himself, above all, to be a man of integrity. Once his word is given a contract is not necessary. Certainly he is loyal. Many of those who supported him during the final period of his time at Pippa Dee are now with him at Next.

Market segmentation

At the heart of the Next success story is the ability to find (or create) financially attractive market gaps and to exploit them to the full. Early, less defined, segmentation aspirations were to sell clothes to the more affluent working women who 'had outgrown Chelsea Girl but didn't want to shop in Marks & Spencer'. Today, segmentation skills and perceptions are more sophisticated and related more clearly to the Next mission. Davies claims . . . 'We like to do things in a certain way – whatever we do. It is a mission'. The mission reflects Davies' own view of how Next should be perceived – 'Visionary, different, well-designed and functional, and satisfying a customer need for exclusivity'. The approach underlying Next activity extends to the impressive village-Head-Office in the Leicester countryside which has been nominated for a special design award. Davies sees his expression of mission permeating the total organisation.

The 'exclusivity' fundamental, however, brings problems to Davies' continuing hunger for growth. Growth and exclusivity do not go hand in hand. Furthermore, existing market players such as Marks & Spencer and newer entrants such as Benetton have all tried to emulate Next's success formulae and to attract growing shares of Next's 'Yuppie-ish' market. Faced with these twin problems, the Next solution appears to revolve around two strategies. On the one hand, growth is being achieved by moves into new areas of business rather than through attempting to create mass markets from existing customer bases. In Davies' words, 'We have moved into different markets so we haven't hit the problems that occur when you go for massive volumes in one market'. On the other hand, the organisation is further segmenting its existing markets. Next itself has recently (1987) been sub-segmented into Next Collection, offering clothes for the traditional Next customer who is primarily looking for stylish workwear and into Next Too, aimed at the Next customer when she is seeking a more casual, less constrained wardrobe.

Ultimately, of course, continuous sub-segmentation ends in a situation where *every* customer is perceived as a market segment – a scenario which will depend upon the ability of store staff to respond to their customers in a very personal manner.

The marketing mix

'At the end of the day, it is about product', says Davies. 'Unless the product is regarded as the central issue in retailing, then retailers having problems will not solve them.' Product attractiveness and basic quality is, of course, essential if the reality of a Next purchase is to meet the customer's expectations.

Product failure destroys the potential effectiveness of other aspects of the marketing mix. 'Unless the products are altered to become attractive, frequent interior design changes are necessary to keep the customers.' Given this basic perception of the importance of product, it is not surprising that the Next organisation works closely with its manufacturers and rather than buying in manufacturers' creations, takes responsibility itself for designing the clothes that are expected to prove attractive to next year's customer. Once again, the offer of exclusivity produces problems. Next store staff expect – and deal with – the hassle of customers complaining that lack of availability of garments 'similar to my friend's' is due to organisational inefficiency.

Exclusivity and product quality, however, do attract value-adding price premiums. Next's pricing polices have, reputedly, been deliberately set at Marks & Spencer type prices, plus at least 10%.

Selling staff are instructed that 'Next is about personal service. Self-service is what you get at supermarkets'. The Next Selling Skills package is supplemented by 12 weeks' training for Next's 'Sales Consultants'. Body language secrets and those of the best way to approach customers are features of training programmes.

Retailing depends, to some large extent, on how property developers see the value of a site. The strength of sites held by Hepworth and Burtons helped both organisations through the leaner years of the late 1970s and early 1980s. The newly enlarged portfolio of properties enables Next senior management to play the chessboard of rearranging the total Next chain location structure. The portfolio is flexible. Market research determines which sites are most suitable for particular categories of Next type customers. For example, if Salisbury's is expected to do better in

Burton-on-Trent than the existing Next for Men store, then Salisbury's will move in and Next for Men will move out. Twelve 'Complete' stores (offering around 25,000 to 40,000 square feet of selling space) were in operation by 1987. These were lighter and bigger than the traditional Next outlets. All offer an uncluttered purchase situation. Effective stock replacement systems facilitate this approach. Staff are encouraged to take pride in their stores – the High Street presence of Next is regarded as the major potential generator of sales. Window displays are designed and changed by a mobile team directed by Head Office although the creative flair of the store staff is put to good use on the internal display areas, giving each site its own subtle personality. The total ambience of the Next purchase experience is intended to provide a marked differentiation from that provided by their 'market trader type' mass market competitors.

Next postcards and diaries, splashed with currently in vogue Next colours, supplement ads placed in well-chosen magazines. Davies, himself, tends to rely on the promotional creativity within Next rather than on that supplied by advertising agencies. Advised to allocate £1m for the initial promotion of Next, he instituted a successful campaign which cost just £80,000. In totality, then, the Next marketing mix aims to achieve what Davies describes as the essence of retailing – creating the right illusions for the customer. The Next purchase experience seems, to date, to have successfully bridged the gap between satisfying the functional clothing requirements of customers and of providing a purchase experience which enables customers to express their own preferred self identities.

Inside the organisation

Davies' own strong philosophies have, not unnaturally, been major influencers in shaping the culture of the organisation. One appropriate maxim for the organisational approach to strategic development seems to be 'Ready, Fire, Aim'. In fact, much thought and evaluation goes into developments underlying the constant change which Davies sees as fundamental to continuing success. '. . . Because we keep developing, we keep changing, and that helps keep the image fresh. The only way forward is to change. But as captives of their own industry most organisations resist change. They defend their one goal lead. They only change when they are going broke, when they are 5–0 down. We mustn't defend Next. There's no sacred cow about Next.' Operationally, of course, such philosophies mean that store fitters, for example, find working to tight deadlines an essential part of their jobs, and middle management is required to demonstrate practically Davies' commendations of strength in depth and capability to handle massive, dynamic growth.

New ways of thinking about the retail industry are encouraged. In order to offer the newly targeted 'Juppies' (junior urban professionals) special attention and new ideas, for example, the organisation has brought in designers who *don't* usually design for children. Next has also avoided manufacturers which specialise in children's fabrics in a bid to develop new products and up-date the image of children's clothing. Concern over this type of approach has, however, been expressed in the context of the organisation's move into jewellery and its 'kicking out' of Combined English Store's jewellery industry experts – despite Next's own lack of in-house expertise in this area. Next might defend itself against such allegations by referring to its track record as a *retailer* – regardless of the goods and/or services being offered. Its retailing mission comes through in George Davies' comments on the move further into the financial services industry . . . 'Most retailers have moved into financial services through the prompting of their accountancy arms. We are doing it as retailers and will treat them like other products we market in the High Street.'

'Closeness to the customer' provides another organisational maxim. In the new children's venture, for example, the emphasis is on understanding the child – not the mother. Next understand that today's kids know their own minds. A range is being created for 12 years old *down* rather than from maternity up, like Mothercare. 'Inside' the organisation, too, includes suppliers . . . 'We've worked and worked at our supply system. We had to find suppliers who think, like us, of the final customer. We are both in it together. It's a very fine balance between buyer and supplier and we can't be dominant.'

Provided personnel operate within the core constraints of putting the company and the customer first, then an aura of informality prevails. Managers and staff talk and *listen* to each other. Head Office provides one canteen, no boardroom and few rules.

Finance

Commercial organisations are judged ultimately on financial performance. On this front Next, once again, shows up well. Its very ambitious programme of development has so far worked successfully. In the five years to 1986, sales have doubled to just under £200m and profits have leapt sevenfold. An investor buying into the company ten years ago will have seen his money increase by around 40 times. Until the more recent heavy acquisition programme, the gearing, too, has always been conservative. A £100m rights issue has paid for the 1986/87 developments and put the organisation into a useful position for progressing into the future. Appendix 15.1 provides more detailed financial performance information.

Future developments

Needless to say, Next has no intention of resting on its laurels. Future developments which seem likely to be pursued include:

★ Moves via agency/franchise arrangements (with Gary Weston of Associated British Foods – with whom George Davies 'gets on very well') into the United States and Canada.

★ Development into the under-25 fashion market – and the inevitable clashes with giants Burtons and Sears.

★ 'Next Gentlemen' and 'Next Ladies' as the organisation seeks to retain its customers as they grow up.

★ The progression of Club 24 to 'licensed deposit taker' status and into mortgage and insurance business.

★ A highly innovatory approach to mail order business.

One thing seems certain for all those associated with Next. A sure answer to the question of 'What Next?' is 'Change – and more change!'

Appendix 15.1   *Next plc – Financial Information*

Consolidated Profit and Loss Account

	Aug 31 1982 (£'000)	Aug 31 1983 (£,000)	Aug 31 1984 (£'000)	Aug 31 1985 (£'000)	Aug 31 1986 (£'000)
Turnover	83,370	98,603	108,331	146,045	190,021
Cost of Sales	73,387	85,542	90,494	119,322	152,984
Gross profit	9,983	13,061	17,837	26,723	37,037
Distribution costs	2,361	2,308	2,746	3,437	5,524
Administrative expenses	5,018	5,405	5,902	7,273	9,750
Associated company's loss	–	–	–	–	294
Non-consolidated subsidiary's profit	(3,644)	(3,926)	(4,475)	(4,740)	(7,044)
Interest	2,388	713	48	690	854
Profit (loss) before tax	3,860	8,561	13,616	20,063	27,659
Corporation tax	–	2,229	5,256	5,833	6,770
Deferred tax	–	54	1,087	2,319	1,060
Overseas tax	–	49	62	85	109
Non-consolidated subsidiary's tax	92	91	113	116	2,648
Prior year tax	(209)	(288)	(1,087)	(82)	(813)
Total taxation	(117)	2,135	5,431	8,271	9,744
Profit (loss) after tax	3,977	6,426	8,185	11,792	17,885
Preference dividends	64	64	64	64	64

Profit after preference dividends	3,913	6,362	8,121	11,728	17,821
Ordinary dividends	1,751	2,438	3,449	5,053	11,460
Extraordinary items	(1,529)	(808)	(461)	(2,147)	563
Retained profit (loss)	3,691	4,732	5,133	8,822	5,798
Holding company	3,363	1,541	2,074	3,127	(10,782)
Subsidiaries	328	3,191	3,059	5,695	16,874
Associated companies	–	–	–	–	(294)
Retained profit (loss)	3,691	4,732	5,133	8,822	5,798

Interest					
Bank loans and overdrafts	1,559	877	199	729	1,545
Medium-term loan	1,020	–	–	67	–
Debentures					
Within 5 years	–	15	8	–	33
After 5 years	102	75	73	73	40
Capitalised	–	–	–	–	(409)
	2,681	967	280	869	1,209
Receivable	(293)	(254)	(232)	(179)	(355)
	2,388	713	48	690	854

Profit before tax is after charging/(crediting) depreciation					
Leasehold property	329	342	391	287	
Plant and vehicles	626	701	850	1,238	5,719
Retail plant and fittings	1,922	2,019	2,382	2,522	
Operating lease rentals					
Plant & Machinery	554	620	623	373	563
Other	–	–	4,269	8,190	11,774
Property repairs and maintenance	438	–	–	–	–
Auditors' remuneration	67	57	69	72	
Directors'					
Emoluments	257	300	340	329	559
Compensation	–	–	–	–	100
Staff costs					
Wages and salaries	16,429	16,833	17,288	20,874	27,488
Social security	1,836	1,590	1,581	1,810	2,076
Pension	450	425	342	327	551
Share scheme	20	20	74	182	237
	18,735	18,868	19,285	23,193	30,352
Average number of employees	4,057	3,858	3,462	4,493	8,193
Corporation tax rate %	–	52	47.9	42.9	37.9

Extraordinary items

Properties realisation	(2,806)	(1,906)	(1,319)	(4,712)	(1,233)
Closure and costs	1,385	1,203	762	4,524	3,019
Interest disposal	–	379	311	–	–
Deferred tax	–	–	(2,312)	–	–
Transfer from reserves	–	–	2,312	–	–
Debenture redemption	(108)	–	–	–	–
	(1,529)	(324)	(246)	(188)	1,786
Taxation	–	(484)	(215)	(1,959)	(1,223)
	(1,529)	(808)	(461)	(2,147)	563

1987 (May) rankings of UK companies by market capitalisation

Rank	Company	Price (p)	Value (m)
103	Royal Bank of Scotland	324	921.1
104	Unigate	398	895.9
105	Next	343	873.8
106	Burmah Oil	502	867.3
107	RMC Group	887	844.4

Appendix 15.2   *Next plc – Organisation Activities – to November 1986*

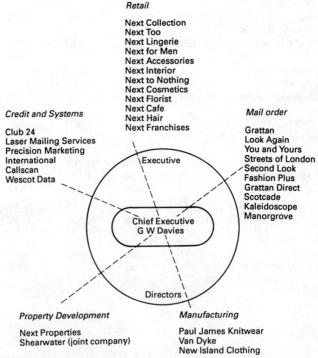

Next Group Activities 1986

Retail

Next Collection
Next Too
Next Lingerie
Next for Men
Next Accessories
Next Interior
Next to Nothing
Next Cosmetics
Next Florist
Next Cafe
Next Hair
Next Franchises

Credit and Systems

Club 24
Laser Mailing Services
Precision Marketing
International
Callscan
Wescot Data

Executive

Mail order

Grattan
Look Again
You and Yours
Streets of London
Second Look
Fashion Plus
Grattan Direct
Scotcade
Kaleidoscope
Manorgrove

Chief Executive
G W Davies

Directors

Property Development

Next Properties
Shearwater (joint company)

Manufacturing

Paul James Knitwear
Van Dyke
New Island Clothing

Retail outlet by activity	Aug 85	Aug 86	Nov 86	1987
Next Too		112	117	
Next Collection	210	109	114	
Next for Men	114	162	174	
Next Lingerie	0	5	42	
Next Accessories (stand alone)	0	3	8	
Next Interior	14	36	40	
Next Cafe	5	9	10	
Next Espresso Bar	1	6	8	
Next Florist	5	8	8	
Next Hairdressers	0	3	3	
Next to Nothing	2	15	23	
Hepworths	84	0	0	
	435	468	547	
More recent additions:				
– Salisburys				150
– Zales/Collingwood/Weir				265
– Paige				208

Appendix 15.3   *Next plc – Some Market Sector Information*

(i) *Mail Order*

Sales rose to £3bn in 1986 after a recession in the early 1980s. This represents 6% of total retail spending. Some forecasters reckon sales in this sector will achieve £4.5bn by 1990. Younger, middle class customers are beginning to show interest in this form of non-shop shopping, although the dominant customer base remains the older, lower class segment. 1986 mail order market shares included:

GUS	42%
Littlewoods	25.3%
Freemans	13.7%
Grattan	10.2%
Empire	6.2%
Other	2.6%

Source: Verdict Research

(ii) *Newsagency Industry*

The market for newsagents shops remains buoyant. Four of the UK's seven largest newsagent chains have changed hands during 1986/87. This bid activity reflects to some extent the fact that newsagents are about the last retailing business to resist conglomeration. Independents still dominate – even the largest operator, W H Smith, only accounts for about 7% of the UK's £8bn annual expenditure on confectionery, tobacco and newspapers. The small man – helped by his family – can still run a shop in a way that bigger chains would find uneconomical. Also the near monopoly of newspaper distribution enjoyed by wholesalers means that new entrants have to buy an existing newsagent, as the wholesalers are reluctant to supply new outlets.

However, while the price of existing newsagent outlets seems set to be maintained at least at existing levels the profitability of the industry will remain unexciting. With two thirds of newsagency sales derived from newspapers and tobacco the industry suffers from declining market demand for both products. Further, newsagents cannot compete through the exercise of purchase muscle power as can their supermarket competitors in the confectionery market.

(iii) *Children's Clothing*

With the children of the 1960s' baby boom now themselves beginning to breed, forecasters are anticipating the growth of the importance of the pre-teen market. In 1986 the children's clothing market was worth £2.2bn. Market shares were estimated as being:

Marks & Spencer	11%
Mothercare (strong in babywear)	9%
British Home Stores	4.5%
Woolworths	3.5%
Boots	3%

Industry players are preparing themselves to take their shares of the growing market. Boots is to spend £100m on its Children's World Venture, Woolworths plans to open 100 kids' stores over the next five years.

The new 'Juppie' generation seems certain to have the freedom to pick and choose.

Appendix 15.4 *The Price and Yields of Prime Retail Space – 1987*

Shop rents	£ per annum	Shop Investment Yields	%
1 New York	297,000	1 Switzerland	3.5
2 Zurich	258,000	2 UK	4.0
3 Geneva	228,000	3 West Germany	5.0
4 London	200,000	4 Australia	6.0
5 Paris	159,500	5 Holland	7.0
6 San Francisco	148,500	5 Italy	7.0
7 Melbourne	137,500	5 Sweden	7.0
8 Brisbane	118,500	5 USA	7.0
9 Sydney	100,000	6 Belgium	7.5
10 Glasgow	100,000	10 France	7.5
(Based on a 1,500 sq ft prime retail unit – city centre)		(Initial purchasing yields on prime retail properties)	

Source: Hillier Parker International Property Bulletin: 1987
Notes:

1 More than 2.2 million people were employed in the 800m square feet of retail property in Britain in 1987.

2 Annual retail sales value stood at more than £80bn per year.

3 Prime office buildings remain the major attractors of property investment. Shop properties had, however, moved into second place (from under a fifth in the early 1980s to well over a third of total property investment by 1987).

4 61m square feet of out-of-town retail schemes had been put before planners by the end of 1986.

16 · Media extracts on the Sinclair Organisation

Bill Richardson and David Roberts

The following are newspaper extracts on the Sinclair organisation which appeared between mid-1984 and 1986.

Advocates of "commuter cars," be they electric or petrol-engined, argue – quite correctly I am sure – that 86 per cent of all car journeys in Britain involve a 4/5-seat vehicle carrying only one or two people. They point out, too, that the average car journey is only six miles. From which they deduce there must be a pent-up demand for a two-seat car with low running costs even though (in the case of the battery electric) it has a refuelling range of no greater distance than a Mini will run on a gallon of petrol. Then it has to go on charge for about eight hours before it can run again, whereas the Mini or the Fiat 126 can go from Lands End to John o' Groats if needs be, which makes it a better buy because it is a more flexible product.

How many readers of this column would buy a battery electric with a 50-mile range as a second car? I should like to know. So, I am sure, would Sir Clive Sinclair. If you would buy one, why? For environmental reasons, for economy, because they are so easy to drive?

Sinclair's TV: So small it isn't there

by Victor Smart

SIR CLIVE SINCLAIR is battling to salvage his two-inch flat-screen television, which has proved a spectacular flop since its launch last September amid a blaze of publicity.

The £79.95 television hailed as 'a major breakthrough,' is the latest in a long line of projects which potential customers have been unable to lay their hands on.

Last week the Office of Fair Trading criticised Cambridge-based Sinclair Research for making unrealistic delivery claims for its ZX series of home computers. Even the recently launched QL home computer has suffered substantial delivery delays.

Sinclair said yesterday of his television project: 'We are now very pleased with progress at the tube plant, although it will be later in the year before we can move into volume. Despite the delays, we are still far ahead technically of the Japanese.'

He added: 'We are quite certain we will be dominant in the market place.'

Developed at a cost of £4 million, the miniature television is the first to work from a single silicon chip, and uses an advanced tube design. Production was planned to run at 10,000 units a month by the end of 1983, and the television was expected on the High Street by mid-1984. Sinclair was confident that it would eventually sell up to one million sets a year worldwide. Sir Clive maintains that the project has only been delayed by six months.

But promotion has had to be virtually abandoned, and only 'a few thousand' have been sold since the launch. Despite the lack of advertising and the fact that Sinclair Research's number in Cambridge is now ex-directory, callers who telephone the company's distributors, GSI at Camberley, are told that orders cannot be met for two to three months.

Production of the television, which was claimed at the time of the launch to be less than one-third the price of its nearest competitor, is split between four companies. Timex makes the low power consumption tube; Ferranti the novel chip; AB Electronics the sophisticated tuner; and Thorn EMI's Ferguson and Timex are responsible for final assembly.

Sinclair hopes to announce shortly that it has overcome the formidable problems, and that the television will be in shops in quantity later this year. The flat screen set is Sinclair's second attempt to make money from a miniature television – the first failed to sell.

Sinclair's institutional shareholders are likely to closely question Sir Clive at the company's annual general meeting in the autumn. Sinclair will claim that the television 'will be a very significant contributor to turnover and profits next year.'

From: *The Observer*, 24 June 1984

Sinclair float delayed

by STEVE VINES and MICHAEL GILLARD

Despite the company's evident success as a microcomputer innovator and designer of new electronic products, it has been plagued by production difficulties and heavily criticised for delivery delays. Last financial year (ending 31 March) was particularly bad. Two major products, the up-market QL computer and the pocket flat screen TV, were announced with great fanfare and then failed to reach customers without considerable delay.

Searle acknowledges that there is disquiet about Sinclair's financial performance among the company's institutional investors who own 10 per cent of the shares. But he says, 'The problem with the institutions is that they don't see all our business. When they see the results for 1983–84, they will not, for example, include QL sales. The picture they are looking at is out of date

and so different from six months later. If they go on that, I can understand that they may be unhappy.'

Sinclair's strategy, says Searle, is to look to the long term, sacrificing short term profit for sustained growth. But he admits 'it is very difficult to convince people that we're doing all the right things and that they shouldn't worry about last year.'

He points out that Sinclair shares were bought in 1983 on the basis of a very speculative profit earnings ratio. 'There's not a damn thing any of our shareholders should worry about, there's just a gap between information and knowledge,' Searle declares.

Such views are hardly likely to reassure unit trusts, insurance companies and investment trusts who paid £34 for their shares last year.

Then they rushed to buy on City projections that Sinclair could produce profits of at least £25 million in the year now ended – and over £30 million in the current year.

Now the expectation is that, at very best, profits for last year will be little different to last year's £14 million. More likely, they will be lower.

Customers complaining about delays in getting hold of new Sinclair products are also given an assurance by Searle. Following criticism by the Advertising Standards Authority, Sinclair reaffirmed its policy of not taking customers' money for products which were not available. Searle has gone a step further by saying, 'We will make no promises on delivery which we can't keep.'

From: *The Observer*, 5 August 1984

Sinclair denies market collapse

By Jason Crisp

SINCLAIR RESEARCH, the troubled home computer group, yesterday strongly denied that the British home computer market had collapsed and predicted only a small fall in sales this year.

At the same time, the company confirmed that it was seeking to raise £10m to £15m "to fund long-term growth and restructuring plans" and that a new chief executive was being sought to replace Sir Clive Sinclair, founder and largest shareholder, who would remain chairman.

The company is particularly keen to reassure potential investors that the home computer market is not finished.

There is considerable dispute over the market. Some surveys

show that sales last year were slightly higher than in 1983, though this is partly because there was considerable unsatisfied demand just before Christmas 1983 which resulted in higher sales in early 1984.

Nearly half the home computers bought in Britain are purchased in the final three months of the year. Demand in this critical pre-Christmas period last year was lower than in 1983. As a result Sinclair Research ended the year with stocks worth £34m, which have now been reduced to £30m.

Yesterday the company predicted the total home computer market this year would be 1.2m units compared with

1.5m last year and said it had 40 per cent of the total.

The company is to start discussions with potential industrial partners which may take a substantial minority stake.

It said it could take up to two months to find suitable investors in the company. Its cash flow problems have been temporarily solved as its major creditors, Thorn-EMI and Timex, which make its computers, had accepted a two-month delay in payments.

Sinclair Research does not appear to be in as difficult a position as was Acorn, the other leading UK home computer company, earlier this year when it had to be rescued by Olivetti of Italy.

Sinclair's woe
by MICHAEL GILLARD

SUCH is the gloom among the 100 City investors in Sir Clive Sinclair's *Sinclair Research* there are now fears that profits for the year ended in March may not reach £5 million. That compares with £14.28 million in 1983–84 and £7.9 million in the nine months to end-December.

It is believed that Sinclair lost money in January, probably in February, and possibly in March. All of the problems that hit profits earlier in the year have continued, in some cases even more so. Falling sales, the price-cutting war and dissatisfied customers returning faulty personal computers.

Even profits of £5 million – seem by some as perhaps the best to expect – are a long, long way from the hopes of more than £30 million anticipated at the time of the share placing by merchant bankers Rothschilds two years ago.

Since then the original investors, mainly insurance companies and unit trusts, have seen the capitalisation of the Sinclair company fall from £136 million to £40 million.

For those institutions locked into Sinclair Research and showing a loss of at least £24 on shares that cost £34 each at the time of the £13.6 million placing there is little they can do but wait and hope. With only 10 per cent of the shares they have little means of influencing the founder, Sir Clive Sinclair, who controls the rest. Indeed the great inventor has shown little interest in their views. The two meetings with his shareholders since 1983 have been more at their insistence rather than at his invitation.

All of which makes any question of a stock market flotation academic until Sinclair Research's profit picture and Sir Clive Sinclair's relationship with the City improve.

From: *The Sunday Telegraph*, 21 April 1985

Sinclair cuts production of C5 by 90%
BY OUR MOTOR INDUSTRY CORRESPONDENT

PRODUCTION of the Sinclair C5 electric vehicle has been cut from 1,000 to 100 a week because of poor initial sales.

Only 10 of the original 100 employed on the C5 production line at the Merthyr Tydfil, mid-Glamorgan, factory began work again yesterday following a three-week halt for modifications to a gearbox component on vehicles in stock.

The rest have been transferred to washing machine production in the Hoover factory which makes the C5 under contract for Sinclair.

Mr Bill Bish, works convenor, said production had been cut to one-tenth of the original level. Sinclair Vehicles would not be drawn on details but acknowl-edged that it would be "operating at a reduced rate to allow supply to adjust current stock levels."

It is estimated that about 3,000 of the £399 three-wheeled vehicles are unsold. "We will be reviewing production requirements more or less on a weekly basis and expect a rise in sales now the weather is improving," Sinclair said.

By the end of February about 5,000 on the vehicles had been sold through an initial mail-order campaign after the January launch. In March the C5 went on retail sale and nearly 500 outlets stock it.

Sir Clive Sinclair said last night: "Sales have not been entirely up to expectations. We have taken longer to establish ourselves in the retail market than we hoped. But sales are now rising steadily and we are confident of a high level of demand for the vehicle."

Sinclair Vehicles is separate from Sir Clive's electronics and computers group. Its original target was to produce 100,000 of the C5s, which need no road tax or insurance, a year.

Sinclair insisted yesterday that it remained optimistic, and was confident of reaching the original sales target. However, some Sinclair executives acknowledge that a spring launch might have been more successful than a January one because weather conditions would have been more suitable for the open-topped vehicles.

From: *The Financial Times*, 23 April 1985

Sinclair under pressure as Acorn details £20m loss

By Bill Johnstone and Graham Searjeant

The principal creditors of Sinclair Research are expected to press this week for a guaranteed reduction of the £15 million debts owed to them in the wake of a £10 million contract for Sinclair to supply Dixons, the high street retailers, with 160,000 home computers and televisions from stock.

News of the order was rushed out on Friday after Mr Robert Maxwell withdrew the offer by his Hollis group to take control of Sinclair via a £12 million cash injection.

The main trade creditors are Thorn-EMI, AB Electronics and Timex, which subcontract manufacturing of Sinclair products.

Together with the bank creditors, Barclays and Citibank, they will be anxious to be convinced that Sinclair has not merely bought time but that, as Sir Clive Sinclair has claimed, "It has become clear to all parties, as a result of recent sales successes, that the proposed refinancing of Sinclair Research is not necessary".

Three months ago Thorn-EMI, which is owed £7 million, disclosed that it had extended Sinclair's credit by two months because of the company's inability to pay. The two other manufacturers followed suit. Timex later sold its stock of 60,000 Spectrum computers abroad.

Meanwhile the difficulties of the home computer market are shown starkly in a circular sent to shareholders of the rival Acorn Computers, giving details of a £4 million capital injection by Olivetti which became necessary after £12 million raised mainly from Olivetti in March proved insufficient to cope with the group's liquidity problems.

The circular reveals that Acorn's turnover tumbled to £22.9 million in the first six months of the year compared with £55 million in the previous half year. Unaudited accounts indicate that Acorn made an operating loss of £9.8 million between January and June and a loss of £14.1 million after interest and exceptional write-offs.

This makes a total pretax loss of £20.6 million for the year to June. And that is with the benefit of agreement wih the BBC to waive all but £330,000 out of royalty debts of £2.2 million for the use of its name on Acorn computers.

During the last three months of the financial year, Acorn's turnover was running at only 30 per cent of the same period in 1984 and some of its debtors went into receivership or were slow to pay.

The document makes it clear that Acorn would have gone into receivership without the new injection of cash, which values Acorn shares at only 1p.

Mr Brian Long, Acorn's new managing director, said yesterday that sales of the basic BBC computer had trickled along at a good rate since the year end.

There was evidence that destocking by retailers of home computers had stopped but there was no evidence of any upsurge in sales.

● Output of semi-conductors in Kyushu, Japan's "silicon island" dropped in May for the first time. Leading manufacturers are laying off part-time workers and not replacing employees who leave for the first time since setting up in the island in the mid-1970s.

From: *The Times*, 12 August 1985

Creditors wait on Sinclair

by LINDSAY VINCENT

CREDITORS of *Sinclair Research*, the troubled home computer enterprise, have undertaken to continue to support the company until the end of the year.

It was agreed at a meeting last week to extend credit lines for the next few months, and reassess the position in the light of the all-important Christmas season. The main creditors are Timex, Thorn-EMI and AB Electronics. The bankers are Barclays and Citibank.

After Robert Maxwell withdrew his 'rescue' bid for the company two weeks ago, Sinclair reached an important deal with Dixon Group. The retailer has agreed to buy £10 million of the company's £30 million of unsold stocks and promote them heavily in the weeks leading up to Christmas. The Dixon order has stimulated interest from other retailers such as Boots and W.H. Smith. There had been a marked recovery in demand, but there is no certainty that it will be sufficiently sustained to avoid a restructuring of the company's capital and debts. This is expected after Christmas.

Creditors still dispute whether Sir Clive Sinclair, the company's founder, is the right man to be running the business.

Meanwhile, Sinclair has stepped up the home computer war by slashing the price of its top model, the floundering QL. The price has been halved from £399 to £199.95. The irony is that this price cut may affect sales of the best-selling Spectrum model.

From: *The Observer*, 1 September 1985

From: The Financial Times, 15 October 1985

John Griffiths on the failure of the *Sinclair* vehicle C5's road to the receiver

SIR CLIVE SINCLAIR launched his C5 electric tricycle on January 10 this year with a ringing declaration that the C5 heralded the fact that "by the turn of the century the petrol engine will be seen as a thing of the past."

Ten months later, it is Sir Clive's creation which is a thing of the past, unless some "white knight" comes to the rescue with enough in his saddlebags to pay off creditors and get production going again.

Mr David Saute and Mr Anthony Locke, the receivers from Begbies, the London accountancy firm which yesterday began the task of unscrambling the C5 company's affairs, see the launch as symbolising much of what was wrong with the project.

It took place, with much ballyhoo, before the world's media at Alexandra Palace in London, with "test drives" inside and through the hilly grounds which were covered in snow and ice. The few hardy journalists who ventured out on the roads returned shivering and dubious about the C5's abilities in such harsh conditions.

It was the worst possible timing to launch what was proclaimed to be a serious, road-going vehicle – and one which could be driven, without a licence or insurance, by 14-year-olds.

As sales failed resolutely to take off, Sir Clive himself, by early summer was prepared to concede that the C5's reception might have been better had the launch been delayed until the kinder weather of spring.

By then, the writing was on the wall.

"The vehicle appears to have been marketed wrongly," Mr Saute observed discreetly yesterday. "It was presented as serious transport, when perhaps it should have been presented as a luxury product, an up-market plaything."

Sir Clive's appointment of receivers, however, climaxed a seemingly endless catalogue of adversity for the machine, which in the last few weeks has been offered for sale by the Comet retail chain for £189, including accessories. That is well under half the original asking price of £399 for the basic model.

Sir Clive put £7m into the venture personally. Hoover also assumed some of the risk in setting up the production facility at its Merthyr Tydfil, South Wales, washing machine plant.

By the end of last year the first vehicles were coming off an assembly line capable of producing 180,000 C5s a year, and with optimists suggesting eventual capacity for 800,000.

A few days before the launch, however, the C5 was already embroiled in controversy. The British Safety Council published a report suggesting that while the vehicle was not intrinsically unsafe, there was a potential safety hazard in terms of its visibility to other road users. Sir Clive announced his intention to issue a writ, but one was never served.

The 15-mph "trike" ran into a barrage of post-launch criticism, not least that its claimed 20-mile range was over-optimistic.

By the end of January, with the company reluctant to admit sales figures, it was announced that plans for a second assembly line were being "postponed."

By mid-February, however, it was claiming that more than 5,000 had been sold. Figures issued by the receivers yesterday show the total to be 4,500.

In March, Sir Clive said the C5 would be followed in a few years by the C10, a 30 mph two-seater, and by 1990 a four-seater "capable of 80 mph and with a range of hundreds of miles."

By the last week of April, production was being cut from 1,000 a week, already well under target, to 100. The 100 Hoover employees who had been assembling the C5 were cut to about a dozen.

At the same time, the vehicle fell foul of the Advertising Standards Authority which ruled that a number of claims made for it could not be substantiated.

By then, the more than 400 retail outlets, including Comet and some Woolworth stores, selling the machines were becoming disillusioned.

In May, a week after the production controller at Merthyr Tydfil had been made redundant, Sir Clive admitted that stocks, at 6,000, were twice previously disclosed levels.

Perhaps the most serious blow to the project's credibility was dealt in July, when Hoover issued a writ against Sir Clive personally, seeking more than £1.5m for work carried out on the C5.

The writ was never served, and while Hoover would not comment on the issue yesterday, Sinclair Research, Sir Clive's electronics concern, said yesterday the issue had now been resolved.

The penultimate blow fell in mid-August, when it was disclosed that production of the C5 had ceased.

The receivers were formally appointed last Friday.

Little hope for *Sinclair* creditors

By Patience Wheatcroft

Creditors of Sir Clive Sinclair's collapsed C5 electric car business are angry about the way he may have pre-empted their claims on the assets of the company.

At a creditors' meeting near Coventry, Warwickshire, yesterday it emerged that on April 11, Sir Clive took out a £5 million debenture to cover money that he had put into the company.

The debenture was secured against assets which may now be worth £500,000. Other creditors are owed nearly £1 million.

Ordinary trade creditors are unlikely to recover any of their money from the company. According to the accountants, Touche Ross, which has been appointed liquidator to the company, there is a total deficiency of £6.4 million.

The company, known as Sinclair Vehicles previously, was restructured to leave a sales company which could continue trading, trying to sell the 4,800 C5s which are still unsold. The holding company, renamed TPD,

was put into receivership, and yesterday went into liquidation.

Sir Clive is believed to have put £8.6 million of his own money into the venture, £2.7 million of it being written off before production of the C5 began. He now claims to be owed £5.9 million by the company.

The Inland Revenue is owed £76,000 but the biggest commercial creditor is a London electrical company, Primary Contact.

From: *The Times*, 6 November 1985

Jason Crisp on optimism at a troubled computer company

Sinclair's program for recovery

THERE is remarkable optimism at *Sinclair Research*, considering that the company was on the verge of collapse in the summer. The size of its problems are shown in the report and accounts received by shareholders yesterday, some 10 weeks later than usual.

The bloodbath in the home computer industry – and incidentally semiconductors – has cost Sinclair Research £22.8m in exceptional items, mainly stock write-downs. As a result a modest pre-tax profit of £4.5m has been turned into an £18.3m loss which is alleviated only by a £7.2m tax credit.

But with most of the bad news apparently out of the way, Sir Clive Sinclair, founder and chairman, and Mr Bill Jeffrey, the new managing director who joined from Mars Electronics, both exude a renewed confidence.

Earlier this week, they spent the day with the company's financial advisors N. M. Rothschild discussing how to raise £10m to restore working capital and enable the company to go ahead with a number of product launches next year.

Sinclair's problems originated last year when the industry was highly optimistic that the home computer boom would continue. But the British public only bought 1.4m units, significantly lower than the previous year. Sir Clive comments in his chairman's report: "The retail trade, overreacting to the rising market and the supply shortages experienced in the two preceding years, bought 1.8m machines. The pattern was the same in all major markets last year, and the result was a virtually complete cessation of deliveries to retailers in

the first three months of 1985."

Sir Clive does not say in his report that Sinclair Research – along with its rival Acorn Computers – also greatly overestimated demand. The balance sheet for the year to March 3 shows stocks of £21.3m after making write-downs of £17.5m. Given that there were no sales in the first three months of 1985, one can estimate that Sinclair ended the peak Christmas selling season with five months' stock on its hand, on the basis of past demand.

Since the market has fallen this year and the business is so seasonal, the company probably will not get all its stocks right until about March 1986. "We're eating into stocks quite dramatically now," said Mr Jeffrey. The company's most important product, the Spectrum home computer has been selling so well that manufacturing has been restarted.

The stock problems caused a cash flow crisis this summer, which meant it had to be rescued by its main creditors, Thorn EMI, AB Electronics, Barclays Bank and Citibank. It later led to an abortive £12m rescue bid by Mr Robert Maxwell, publisher of the Mirror Group of newspapers.

But when Mr Maxwell abandoned Sir Clive in August, the company had just clinched a £10m deal with Dixons which enabled it to limp on unaided.

There have been a number of changes at Sinclair Research since the crisis, aimed at converting a mercurial but haphazardly-run company into a more professionally managed organisation. Sales and marketing have been reorganised and the

concept of "brand management" introduced. The already-small staff of 120 has been cut and the board reorganised and sharply reduced in size. New professional managers have joined to beef up quality control, engineering and financial systems.

Assuming the company succeeds in raising the £10m it needs, it plans to launch new products next year. One of the main strategies is to preserve its position as the dominant supplier in the UK home computer market. Next year should be better for Sinclair.

Sinclair will also move towards the business market with a portable computer – known as Pandora – which Sir Clive promises for late next year.

The Pandora will have a 12 inch flat screen cathode ray tube, like the much smaller one used in the Sinclair pocket TV. "It will also not cost a penny more than the equivalent desk-top machine," said Sir Clive.

Sir Clive admitted yesterday that his hope that the pocket TV might become as popular as the transistor radio was not realised.

It has clearly been an exceptionally difficult year for Sir Clive who has also seen a substantial part of his personal fortune disappear with the collapse of his other company, Sinclair Vehicles. Even his salary at Sinclair Research has been cut from £77,000 to £53,000.

Clearly, the company will be rather different, both in terms of management and size. Sir Clive concentrates on the technology, leaving company management to Mr Jeffrey. Turnover will, it is clear, be substantially down on the £102.8m achieved last year.

From: *Financial Times*, 30 November 1985

Midas who lost his touch

By Alan Cane

SIR CLIVE SINCLAIR seemed in June 1983 to be the very epitome of the New Elizabethan Technologist – innovative, buccaneering and successful.

Knighted by an admiring Mrs Thatcher, he was also named "Young businessman of the year," his profits guaranteed that the City was happy to indulge this Midas of the microchip. He had been right about calculators and computers. Perhaps he was also right about pocket television, wristwatch radios and electric cars.

He seemed to many to herald a renaissance for a UK industry in decline powered by the union of traditional British inventiveness with the new information technology. Within three years, however, that silicon vision had crumbled into worthless sand.

An advanced home computer took an interminable time to reach the market. The pocket television failed to excite. And the electric car emerged as a somewhat ridiculous battery operated trike, sowing powerful doubts about Sinclair's competence in his investors' minds.

Finally, overwhelmed by debt and unsold stock, he was forced to sell his computers, patents and even his birthright, the Sinclair name, Mr Alan Sugar's Amstrad scooped the lot for a mere £5m.

The fall of Sinclair is well documented. Explanations for why a company and an individual in which the government of the day, had placed such faith and which seemed to represent the aspirations of an entire nation should have come to such a sorry pass are less easy to untangle.

Two computer journalists, Mr Ian Adamson and Mr Richard Kennedy, in a new study* suggest the fault lay principally with Sinclair's obsessions.

Far from being the prolific inventor of popular acclaim, they argue, Sir Clive had actually produced comparatively few ideas of value in his 30 years of professional activity.

"While other unsung inventors produced such things as the computerised running shoe (Sir Clive, a marathon runner, might have been expected to come up with that one!), the fingertip pulse monitor, the pocket computer database and a plethora of microchip-dependent products sold by mail order and generating quiet profits for their producers, Sir Clive puts his greatest energies into his obsessions," they write.

Adamson and Kennedy make their points strongly, but for me their essay and their principal conclusion is spoiled by an undercurrent, running through the book, of pleasure at his downfall. *Schadenfreude*, as the immensely well read Sir Clive would no doubt delight in telling them.

To be fair, Sinclair invites such treatment. He gives few interviews and writes little but when he does, the impression of overweening self-regard, the anxiety to place the blame for his failures elsewhere, makes him easy meat for his detractors.

What he desires above all else, it seems, is recognition as an inventor of repute. But while he is a master of the language of the electronics specialist – "technobabble" as one critic put it unkindly – which endears him to his own technical staff, Mr Adamson and Mr Kennedy are right to question the popularly-held belief that he is a great inventor and computer genius.

Nevertheless, the City, the politicians and the public found the image of Sinclair the inventor and scientist plausible. The professionals thought otherwise. Even when he was riding high on the success of the nicely styled "Executive" calculator, the experts were not impressed. "Sinclair? Forget it. He is just an assembler" one said in 1975 recommending against Sinclair calculators in favour of nicely-engineered US or Japanese machines.

So Sinclair's reputation as an inventor is open to doubt. By his own admission he is no businessman and the evidence from his shoddily constructed, unreliable products (witness the rate of returns on most of them), indicates he is no engineer.

This is hardly the material of which myths are made. So what was at the root of Sir Clive's popular acclaim? It seems that the British public was willing to credit him with the kind of reputation he craved, because of a national willingness to believe in the brilliance of madcap inventors while affecting contempt for the professional engineer.

It has to be said that it takes no great inventiveness to dream up gadgets like pocket calculators or television sets. The science fiction writers have done it all before. Neither does it take that much ingenuity these days to design a simple microchip-based machine like a home computer. The semiconductor manufacturers have done all the work in designing and fabricating the chip.

But it does take engineering skills of a high order to make such a product to the required quality and to the right price. Sinclair ensured that the price was right, but to do so he compromised the engineering so badly and so often that Sinclair became a byword for poor quality.

The evidence is unshakeable. Calculators blew up in the pockets of their prestigious owners (one was a British ambassador) because Sinclair skimped on the quality of the metal connectors.

The C5, the disastrous electric trike, had a tendency to run out of juice at the first set of traffic lights.

The most depressing aspect of the whole business is that Sir Clive has never shown any signs of learning from his past mistakes and the British public and its government has never shown any signs of graduating from its worship of the gifted amateur inventor to an appreciation of real engineering skills.

Sir Clive, indeed, seems quite irrepressible. Free of debt through the Amstrad deal, he is working on a cheap portable pocket telephone (will it blow up in the pocket like his calculators?) He is planning a portable computer (will it run for more than a few minutes without a change of batteries?).

In his youth, Sinclair eschewed university, arguing that the electrical engineering courses then available had little to offer him.

He was wrong. If he had learned little he did not already know about electronics he might have at least picked up some common sense engineering.

The UK has always had talented inventors. Playing "Dr Who," the eccentric time-travelling scientist of television fame, is virtually a national obsession. It is the leap from talented hobbyist to professional engineer that is hard.

Sir Clive Sinclair still has to make that leap. In their turn, the British public and its government still has to understand and respect what is meant by professional engineering.

Sinclair and the "Sunrise" Technology, Penguin Books, £3.95, paper back.

17 · Storehouse

Glyn Owen

This case study, prepared from published sources, is intended for class discussion and not to illustrate either good or bad management of the organisation.

In January 1986, Terence Conran reached the zenith of his career to date. His Habitat stores group had absorbed Mothercare in 1982 and was now to merge with British Home Stores to create, in Storehouse plc, one of the UK's top retail chains. But by late 1987 Storehouse was at the centre of a whirlpool of actual and rumoured takeover bids. After a cash offer from property company Mountleigh was abandoned, Storehouse found itself facing a bid from Benlox, a tiny engineering company with no retailing experience. How was it that the genius of British retailing could be threatened with the break-up of his company and his own deposition by a small company with no cash?

Terence Conran was born in 1931. He started his career as a freelance furniture designer and established Conran Associates, a design company, in 1956. In 1964 he opened his first shop, which sold a range of furniture, kitchen and tableware and general household goods with the accent on design, quality and style – Habitat was born. By 1978 there were 25 stores in the UK and the beginnings of representation in France and the USA. It was already apparent that internally generated funds were insufficient to sustain expansion and, in late 1981, Habitat shares were floated on the Stock Exchange. Just over 9,000,000 shares were issued at 110p to raise 9.5m net of expenses. Six million pounds was used to repay debt and the remainder was retained for expansion. After the sale, Conran held slightly more than 50% of the shares and he, his family and Habitat executives held over 70%. The issue was successful but not spectacularly so, the shares trading on a p/e of roughly 13–15, high by the standards of the day, but not a glamour rating. (P/e is the ratio of share price to earnings per share. Eps, is total profit (after interest and tax) divided by the number of shares in issue. So if the price of a share is 2 and eps is 10p then p/e is 20. The reciprocal of p/e (1/20 or 5% in this example) is the earnings yield.)

The extent of Conran's ambitions became clear when, only a couple of months after flotation, Habitat made an agreed bid for Mothercare, a specialist retailer of babywear and related products with store chains in both the UK and the US. Mothercare was larger than Habitat which had to issue 62m new shares and £37.5m of loan stock (convertible into a further 26m shares) to buy it. Conran's stake of just over 20m shares represented about 20% of the merged company. Mothercare shareholders held 59% and could increase this to 67% by loan stock conversion. Although the merger was not well received by the City, Habitat's ability to transform Mothercare's profitability was quickly proved and the shares powered ahead from about £1.20 at merger to almost £3 in mid-1982.

HABITAT

Terence Conran opened the first Habitat shop in 1964. It was one fruit of his personal mission to bring good design to UK mass marketed household goods. As a young man in the early fifties he had toured France and been attracted by the solidity and simplicity of French household products, especially kitchenware, compared with their poorly made, if sometimes flashily designed, British counterparts. Habitat design is minimalist: if a thing is designed as simply as possible consistent with doing its job then it is already on the way to looking good. Simple traditional materials are used, wood, ceramics, iron, steel, cotton, and wool, with little plastic, chipboard, or man-made fibre. Colours are predominantly plain with patterns reserved for furniture coverings and similar products. There is a profusion of products in Habitat stores with an even greater variety available to order from well-illustrated catalogues. But there is a definite house style: customers can furnish a room or a whole house from Habitat and be confident that the overall effect will be attractive. For customers uncertain about design principles this can represent a large internal economy.

Good design and materials and wide variety are not cheap. Habitat does not compete in the lowest price ranges, and where it does compete it is usually possible to buy very similar items for less money at other shops. Habitat overcomes this cost/price disadvantage by offering products which look or work better than its rivals', by offering guaranteed quality and the ability to mix and match, and by the signalling advantages of its high-class stores.

In late 1987 Habitat had 52 UK stores. The standard stores, in London and major provincial centres, offer a wide product range and accept orders for products from the Habitat catalogue. Smaller towns have mini stores, sometimes taken over from Mothercare, with a limited range of products. In early 1987 Habitat opened its first giant out-of-town stores, in High Wycombe and Birmingham, intending to have 30 ultimately. These stores have virtually the complete range of products as well as extensive free parking.

Habitat in the UK grew rapidly in its first 20 years and was steadily, if unspectacularly, profitable. But prior to the BHS merger there were signs of worsening gearing as a result of profits being inadequate for expansion.

The first US Habitat – under the name Conran's – was opened in 1977. Establishment of the company in a market where Conran's name was not known and where competition was intense proved an uphill struggle. Losses were made until 1982 and the subsequent profit record was not wholly satisfactory. The limited success achieved resulted from willingness to persist with short-term losses; determination, reflected in heavy investment in warehousing, to reduce costs; and moderate expansion (there were 15 shops by 1987) in a clearly defined area of the north-east USA. Certainly rapid expansion would have been too expensive for Habitat.

Results in Europe were similarly erratic. Habitat started operations in France in the mid-seventies and expanded into Belgium, though it later closed outlets in the latter country. Three shops were opened in Holland in 1987 and start-up losses there held up progress in Europe generally. The international picture is completed by Habitat's franchise operations: by 1987 goods were being sold through 12 stores in Japan and single stores in Iceland, Hong Kong and Singapore.

In 1983 there were two smaller takeovers. In April, Heal's, a high-class family-owned furniture store in London, was purchased for around £5m. It had lost money for years, but conversion of part of its store provided Conran with conveniently located Head Offices. More significantly, Richard Shops was bought from Hanson Trust in October. Hanson had acquired the 200 shop chain when it took over UDS – the old established United Drapery Stores – and had been seeking to dispose of what was certainly not a Hanson type business. Richards was unprofitable, its balance sheet showed negative net worth – a position which was compounded of some £6m of goodwill, shown in the accounts as an asset, was ignored – and was financed mainly by loans from its parent company. Consequently, Conran was able to acquire the equity for next to nothing (about £250,000 was paid) provided he was willing to take over the loans as well. He sought the assistance of Morgan Grenfell, Habitat-Mothercare's merchant bankers, and, in particular, of Roger Seelig, Morgan's representative on HM's Board. Seelig was well known in City circles and a long time friend and business confidant of Conran. Under the Richards takeover deal Morgan and HM each acquired 48%, the remaining 4% being bought by Richards management. HM acquired the right to purchase Morgan's 48% for a small sum (£136,000) and had full management control from the start – Morgan had no interest in running dress shops – but holding only 48% enabled HM to keep Richards and its balance sheet problems at arm's length until it was in better shape. In fact the Morgan shareholding was purchased by Storehouse in 1986 and the management stake in the following year, giving Storehouse 100% ownership.

Habitat-Mothercare's next takeover activity was indirect. In May 1985, Burton made a contested, but ultimately successful, takeover bid for Debenhams. Part of Burton's pitch for control was the Galleria concept – a redesign of Debenhams' rather old-fashioned stores, involving large central stairwells surrounded by selling 'galleries'. Burton did not, however, have convincing expertise in design and marketing of non-clothes lines: this was to be provided by HM. HM was to redesign the Debenhams' stores for Burton and was to have 20% of Debenhams' space for its own products. Furthermore it was to have an option, until the end of 1986, to acquire 20% of Debenhams' equity. Effectively, Debenhams was to be a joint venture with HM as junior partner to Burton. In fact, Burton seems to have gone cool on the idea after the takeover had succeeded, presumably because of the later merger of HM with BHS which was a direct competitor of Burton/Debenhams in a way which HM was not. Following some months of dispute between the two companies a settlement was reached in October 1986. It was announced that Conran Design Group would redesign Burton's flagship Harvey Nichols store and about 400 Burton menswear stores. Storehouse would be offered space in the 66 Debenhams stores as they were refurbished, but only 10% of the total and only for non-BHS merchandise. The equity purchase option was not to be exercised.

MOTHERCARE

Mothercare had 236 stores in the UK, 228 in the USA and 38 in Europe at the Storehouse 1987 Balance Sheet date. The company was founded in 1961 by Selim Zilkha to provide one-stop shopping for mothers-to-be and young children. Its main lines were maternity wear, baby furniture, baby clothes, and disposables such as cotton wool and disposable nappies. At first Mothercare grew rapidly assisted by several social trends:

(1) A high birthrate: annual births in the UK rose from about 800,000 per annum in the early fifties to about 950,000 in the mid-sixties.

(2) Increasing affluence, meaning that the amount spent on each child rose sharply.

(3) The increasing number of working women buying rather than making baby clothes and needing somewhere convenient to shop.

In the seventies, Mothercare expanded into Europe, opening
shops in Belgium, Holland, Switzerland and Scandinavia as
suitable opportunities arose, and into the USA, acquiring a 110
strong chain of shops and then expanding organically to about
200. One of Mothercare's strengths in the UK was its centralised,
computer controlled stock and ordering system, installed by
Zilkha well before such things became commonplace. This was
well suited to the UK operation which had many relatively large
stores in a small geographical area but less suited to Mothercare's
small and scattered US shops.

By the late seventies, Mothercare's profits were falling. Births
in the UK fell to a low of 657,000 in 1977, and there was a
corresponding lagged decline in the population aged between 0
and 5 years. Other firms were invading the Mothercare market:
Boots with 'BabyBoots' and supermarkets with disposable nappies
for instance. Similar trends abroad, where Mothercare was
weaker in the market-place, led to losses which were a further
drain on the UK operation. Habitat's 1982 merger proposal was
therefore welcomed by Zilkha who wished to withdraw from
business life and felt that Conran might revitalise Mothercare.

Mothercare's revival under Habitat control resulted from
improved marketing, an increased birthrate, and realisation of the
virtually unlimited possibilities for related diversification within
Mothercare. The rather aggressive white and orange corporate
colours were replaced with pastel shades; maternity and children's
clothes were made more fashionable both in design and in
material. Crucially, the range of goods sold was extended: the
largest Mothercare stores were given shoe shops, clothes for
children up to 11, and a range of toys of the conventional and
'early learning' types. The range of 'hardware' also expanded as
parents' needs became more sophisticated, calling for in-car baby
furniture, purpose-built drawers, much more elaborate baby baths
and so on. Many shops have crèches and an overall ambience
which reconciles the customer to paying, admittedly for
differentiated merchandise, more than the cost of similar goods
elsewhere. Smaller stores were extended, sold and replaced with
larger stores, or transferred to Habitat for use as limited range
stores in smaller towns. The one failure was the 'Now' chain of
teenage fashion shops. Intended as a junior version of Next or
Benetton, Now soon built up to a 28 shop chain, but never came
near to making a profit and was closed at a cost of some £6m.

In the USA, the attempt to compete head-on with major
retailers in the sale of heavily discounted branded goods was
abandoned, Mothercare turning to higher margin speciality lines.
Centralised control also went, being replaced by autonomous

regional managements. In Europe, unprofitable stores in
Scandinavia were closed.

The success of the initial strategy is demonstrated by an 82%
rise in sales and a 148% rise in profit between 1983 and 1986.
But 1986 was a peak year. Installation difficulties with the new
computerised stock control system and its associated warehouse
reduced profits by 11% in 1987. In the half-year to 19 September
1987 Storehouse had a potential major disaster on its hands as
profits plunged a further 27%. Many stores had to resort to direct
orders to suppliers as the central system virtually broke down.
Far from this costly investment improving profits, it had led to a
dramatic deterioration in performance.

Also in mid-1985 came the start of Conran's most important move yet:
merger with British Home Stores. The familiar high street chain had
substantially improved its performance in recent years with the help of
Conran Design Group. It was now steadily profitable and effectively nil-
geared. But it was widely perceived as a second best to Marks & Spencer,
and an attempted diversification into food lines, which had done so much
for M&S was proving disastrous. The potential for growth in traditional
operations was slight and its stores were outdated. In September 1985
Storehouse was incorporated, with BHS and HM each having 50% of the
(then negligible) share capital. By November merger terms had been
agreed and were recommended to shareholders by the two boards of
directors and their merchant bankers. BHS and HM shares would be
exchanged for Storehouse shares on terms which, allowing for conversion
of HM loan stock, would give existing BHS shareholders about 55% of
Storehouse and HM shareholders 45%. Conran's personal stake would
be about 7%. Shareholders accepted the recommendations by over-
whelming majorities and Storehouse started trading on 6 January 1986.

The strategy underlying the merger was set out in letters from the
chairmen to their own shareholders and in a joint letter from them to all
shareholders. Mere scale was likely to improve the Group's bargaining
strength vis-à-vis suppliers and in competing for prime sites; it would also
improve the ability of the Group to develop businesses such as Habitat's
overseas operations.

There were also expected to be savings from electronic retailing
systems and from more efficient distribution. Most importantly, Habitat's
design skills were to be applied to BHS.

The Storehouse strategy

Conran's design mission is education as well as profit orientated:

'Tastes are shaped by what people are offered. Good taste can be acquired.' – Conran (*The Times*, 17 November 1987.)

This autocratic view is reflected in Conran's management style: he takes many decisions himself, even on quite routine matters, and, where he does delegate, it is to individuals rather than to committees. One of his first moves following the merger was to appoint Jan Kern to effective control of the crucial clothing fashion area of the BHS operation. The idea of having a single person in charge of the overall appearance of a clothes store's fashions had worked brilliantly at Next where Conran, as Chairman of Hepworth, had put George Davies in control: and he meant to repeat this success. Designing and organising production and delivery of mass market fashions is time-consuming – especially when a total look is sought – and decisions must be taken well in advance. This means that trends in fashion must be foreseen where possible and Kern seemed to succeed in doing this (*The Times*, 17 November 1987).

Supplementing Kern's fashion activities were a major redesign of BHS stores in September 1986; and utilisation of space released by the ending of food sales for higher margin lines.

The second major leg of the Storehouse strategy was concerned with distribution and stock control. It was, in principle, easy to see how computer technology could effect enormous cost savings compared with conventional systems. Customer purchases could be recorded electronically at point of sale and this information transferred to a central warehouse. Information on delivery times from warehouse to store, and from supplier to warehouse; on transport fixed and variable costs; on sales rates for every line in every store; and, finally on the costs of holding stocks, in terms of interest and space costs, would enable computers to establish cost-minimising patterns of orders and deliveries. Combined with the latest warehouse technology, permitting random storage of goods controlled by electronic memory of their location, a system could be created under which the whole process of getting different lines from many suppliers to many stores could be carried on, together with its associated paperwork, virtually without human intervention. The savings would appear as lower stock carrying costs; the ability to carry a wider variety of lines; fewer stockouts, and, most importantly for Storehouse, the release of large amounts of in-store space previously used for warehousing.

In pursuit of this strategy, Storehouse built three very large warehouses for Mothercare, Habitat and the US operation. Together with their associated computer systems, in and out of store, this accounted for most of Storehouse's £113m investment programme for the year to 31 March 1987.

Storehouse's first result, for the year to 31 March 1986 (actually covering less than three months of the merged company's existence), were reported in June 1986 and not well received:

'Rather than the Conran magic adding some investment sparkle to the staid but solid BHS, the merger has been sized up as one of those alliances in which the more brilliant partner is held back by the more homely virtues of the other. Rumours that the two management teams were slow to gel have been no help but they do not wholly account for the 20% by which Storehouse has underperformed its sector.' (Lex, *Financial Times*, 6 June 1987.)

BRITISH HOME STORES

The backbone of BHS's business was sale of men's, women's and children's clothes through some 130 stores. In this it resembled its much larger rival Marks & Spencer, though it had traditionally suffered from a downmarket image compared with the latter. Nonetheless, BHS has benefited from its strength in the lighting and restaurant businesses. BHS has long been market leader in UK domestic lighting and, despite competition from a variety of other stores, infrequent purchases, leading to consumer inexperience, and a degree of monopoly power have led to high profits. BHS restaurants provided self-service meals in a clean and pleasant atmosphere. They appeal to people, often middle-aged women, who want an inexpensive sit-down lunch but do not wish to use pubs or fast food outlets.

BHS did badly in the seventies, but its performance was greatly improved in the eighties by Dennis Cassidy, the new Chief Executive. He concentrated on efficiency improvements reflected in an average 11% annual increase in profit per square foot of selling space over the three years prior to the creation of Storehouse. Although Cassidy succeeded in making the group very profitable and cash rich, he was unable to expand its size. Most large towns already have a branch, and the UK market for BHS/M&S type stores is arguably saturated. Moreover, such stores do not seem to do well abroad: even M&S found its West European and North American operations a net drain on company resources and impossible to expand rapidly at acceptable cost. Slow expansion of the number of stores, eg in new shopping centres, and conversion of back-store to selling space produced some growth, as did diversification into an expanded range of household products. But the main diversification, into foodstuffs, was an unprofitable failure, abandoned following the Storehouse merger. Over the period 1982 to 1987, BHS sales grew by just 4.5% per year, a decline in real terms despite booming retail sales generally, though admittedly the figures are distorted by cessation of food sales.

Conran Design Group had advised BHS for years, so merger with Habitat-Mothercare was not a meeting of strangers and the

'Exclamations' redesign of BHS stores in September 1986 brought substantial benefit. There was, however, a conflict between Conran's design-led approach to retailing and Cassidy's efficiency approach – and Conran was in charge. In the *Sunday Times*' words:

'Cassidy retreated to his fiefdom within BHS, implementing effectively the ideas of Conran including the decisions to pull out of food retailing and introduce the 'Exclamations' store display system, but obstructing the full operational merger of the company. Had his acknowledged skills in distribution been brought to bear on Mothercare's problems, there is little doubt that they could have been solved earlier.'

Conflict was exacerbated by the contrast between the continuing profit growth at BHS and difficulties elsewhere in Storehouse, and came to a head with Storehouse's reversal of the decision taken at the time of the merger to make Cassidy Group Managing Director. Cassidy resigned from the Group on 18 September 1987.

Nonetheless, it was recognised that Conran had had only a few months at the helm and that more time was needed. By the time the 1987 results came out it was apparent that expectations were not being fulfilled. Although an advance of 9% (this and following figures for 1987 have been adjusted for 1987 being a 53-week year) in pre-tax profits was scarcely a disaster, it was by no means good in a year of booming retail sales. Moreover, it concealed an 11% fall in profit at Mothercare. Habitat performed stodgily, improving profit by 8%, but BHS, with an advance of 16%, at least matched performance elsewhere in the market. This was certainly not the 'Conran sparkle' investors had expected when Storehouse was formed, and they exerted unremitting selling pressure on the shares, which by April 1987 had underperformed the FT Actuaries All Share index by almost 50% compared with their post-flotation peak. There were, moreover, persistent rumours of difficulties with the new stock control systems and of management problems at BHS: Dennis Cassidy, Chief Executive at BHS, was expected, under the terms of the merger deal, to become Managing Director of Storehouse within a year and this had not happened.

Inevitably speculation started about the possibility of a takeover bid for Storehouse, either as an expansion move by another retailer or as a preliminary to a demerger of Storehouse into its constituent parts. In August the Mountleigh property group announced that it was considering the possibility of a bid for the company. Mountleigh, headed by Tony Clegg, had grown tenfold in size over the year to August 1987 as a result of a series of mergers financed by rights issues. Other possible bidders were Sears, Woolworths, Burton, the US company The Limited, and C & A; and this is not an exhaustive list. Conran, determined to retain independent control of Storehouse, consulted Kleinwort Benson, BHS's merchant bankers, and, less formally, Morgan Grenfell's takeover expert – George Magan.

In mid-September, in-company considerations seemed to take over as Conran's main worry with the resignations of Dennis Cassidy and his deputy at BHS, Colin Williams. In explanation, Conran simply said:

'For some time, we have considered whether Dennis Cassidy should be Managing Director of the Group and Dennis had an expectation that he would. When we decided we should go outside for a candidate, he was very disappointed and decided he should resign.' (*Financial Times*, 19 September 1987.)

A few days later came Mountleigh's bid. Storehouse shareholders were offered, at first, 420p a share raised during negotiations to 445p, valuing the Company at £1.8bn. The offer was in cash, underwritten by Shearson, Lehman, one of the very biggest New York brokers, and would have presaged a demerger operation. Clegg's statement that the offer was conditional on the Board's agreement prompted press speculation that, given Conran's known opposition, the bid was expected to fail, which was strange given the cost of arranging underwriting. All Clegg would say was:

'It is money well spent – this is not the last time we'll need to raise £2bn.' (*Financial Times*, 25 September 1987.)

Jim Power, Storehouse Finance Director, explaining the reasons for rejection of the bid said:

'There was always a profit in it for them, so it couldn't represent full value. That was the fatal flaw.' (*Financial Times*, 25 September 1987.)

Lex was more cautious:

'Storehouse shareholders are nursing a £1 a share loss (the shares had fallen to about 340p). The supposed benefits derived from the Storehouse combination will have to prove that they are worth that difference and sharpish. The company has 15 months of its own three-year restructuring programme to run, but clear signs of superior sales at BHS and an efficiently functioning distribution system for Mothercare will be needed much sooner.' (*Financial Times*, 25 September 1987.)

RICHARDS

When Habitat-Mothercare acquired effective control of Richard Shops in 1983, the chain was unprofitable and squeezed between low-cost general retailers of women's clothes, such as Marks & Spencer, BHS and C&A, and specialist retailers of differentiated fashion clothes such as Principles, Benetton and Next. Acquisition gave Richards access to an improved purchasing function and to the design services of Habitat. Store renovation and introduction to the 'Working woman's wardrobe', a carefully co-ordinated range of reasonably priced clothes designed to mix and match to give a variety of looks from a limited range of clothes, transformed the company into a profitable, if minor, part of the Storehouse Group.

The strategy of concentrating on a particular age range – 25–40 – and on customers able to pay more, though not much more, than average prices, worked at Richards as it had at Habitat. It gave the company a clear position in the market-place: Principles, Next, Benetton and now Richards share a common strategy, however different they might appear to the shopper. In the words of Jan Kern, Managing Director of Conran Design's fashion group: 'Richards is motoring well. It's just a matter of fine tuning'.

HEAL'S

Prior to its takeover by Habitat-Mothercare, Heal's was a family firm with one high-class furniture store in Tottenham Court Road. It had made losses for some years. One of its main attractions was the shop itself, half of which was subsequently converted into well-located head offices for Storehouse. The business was revamped, but the quality image – handmade craftsman-built furniture, advertising in quality magazines, the warrant as suppliers to HM The Queen – was retained. Three new stores, in Guildford, Croydon, and Kingston-on-Thames, were opened. All advertising carried the Heal's message of excellent contemporary design, high quality and a long history as well as product information. In 1986, Heal's design department merged with Conran Associates to form Conran Design Group. Heal's was not expected to make a major profit contribution but its premises and intangible design and marketing benefits were perceived as beneficial to Storehouse.

FNAC

In 1987 Fnac sold a range of video, audio and photographic equipment, together with related records, films, etc, from some 25 shops in France. A major expansion programme was underway both in France and in Belgium. Storehouse, with 20%, was a majority shareholder with GMF, a Paris-based insurance company, having control. The £5m paid for the stake looked expensive in relation to net assets totalling £112m, especially after losses were made in 1984/5. Habitat subsequently became involved in management of Fnac, and the position greatly improved: in 1985/6 turnover was £385m and after tax profits £1.7m. The market value of Storehouse's stake was £16m (Fnac is quoted in Paris) in April 1987. Property was then worth considerably more than book value.

SAVACENTRE

By 1987 SavaCentre operated six hypermarkets in the UK as a 50/50 joint venture with Sainsbury's. The venture was originally between Sainsbury and BHS who had mutual rights to buy the other out in the event of a takeover or merger; but Sainsbury was content to continue with Storehouse as a partner. SavaCentres sold both Habitat and Mothercare products and expanded rapidly in the mid-eighties. The company was originally financed by equity (£16m from each partner) and by equal loans from each partner, but was so successful that the loans were soon repaid. Sales in 1987 were £269m and pre-tax profits £16.9m. The venture was highly successful in its own right and provided increased volume for other parts of Storehouse.

CONRAN DESIGN GROUP

Conran Associates was one of Terence Conran's first business ventures in the fifties, pre-dating Habitat. It merged with Heal's design group in 1986 to form CDG. It carried out a wide variety of design work such as store outfitting, promotional literature, and photographic work. According to the 1987 Storehouse accounts: 'It is one of the most experienced design organisations in the world'. More important than its outside work was its work within Storehouse. It had successively to reposition Mothercare, Heal's, Richards, and BHS as these were acquired as well to participate continuously in the design and marketing of goods sold throughout the Group. This volume of work sometimes strained CDG's resources. CDG's results are determined largely by transfer pricing arrangements.

Only days later came a second demerger bid, this time from Benlox on Sunday, 27 September. Benlox was a small company with a market capitalisation of just £45m. It had various investment dealing and engineering interests, but attention centred on its backers. Dr Ashraf Marwan held 23% of Benlox and its merchant bank adviser, Ifincorp, Earl, was a joint venture between him and a young demerger specialist, Peter Earl. Marwan was married to President Nasser's daughter and was adviser to Anwar Sadat, Nasser's successor as President of Egypt. He thus had connections at the highest level in the Arab world. Since 1983 he had engaged in takeover activity in the London market, notably in House of Fraser, Fleet Holdings, and Extel. The author of the Griffiths inquiry into dealings in House of Fraser shares found that:

'Dr Marwan's evidence . . . did not carry to me the ring of truth.' (*Sunday Times*, 22 November 1987.)

Benlox's Chairman, Andrew Millar, telephoned his all share offer to Conran at home. The offer was to exchange eleven Benlox shares for every two Storehouse. Given Benlox's share price of 91p, this valued Storehouse shares at 501p each, though Benlox would need to issue some 2240m shares in addition to its existing issue of just 49m. The conflicting attitudes of the two men are shown by their reactions to the bid:

'My immediate reaction is disbelief that anything like this can be allowed to happen in this world. It really is very bad news for the City when a company capitalised at just £45m can behave so irresponsibly. Perhaps the Government would like to get around to thinking about it. It can't be welcomed by shareholders and it certainly isn't welcomed by employees. If the shareholders want their company broken up, it is the responsibility of the board to do it, not some small property entrepreneur. At least Mountleigh was offering cash and had taken the trouble to get its bid underwritten. Mr Millar is basically bidding for us with our own shares. What he is putting at risk are his own shares which are of infinitesimal value.' Conran (*The Times*, 28 September 1987).

'This is a very full offer; we expect Sir Terence to view it with respect. Storehouse is a large meal for a company the size of Benlox. But whether one does a £20m demerger or a £2bn demerger, the tenets and discipline are the same. I think it is a very tax-efficient way for shareholders to realise what is otherwise a languishing investment.' Millar (*The Times*, 28 September 1987).

At first, commentators were inclined to treat the bid as frivolous and as having no chance of success, but subsequent events made it more of a threat. First, the stock market crash of late October left institutions holding Storehouse shares worth not much more than half what Clegg had been prepared to pay. Second, Malcolm Parkinson, former Chief Executive of Woolworth Stores and author of its recent revival, had joined the Benlox Board as prospective Managing Director of Storehouse if the bid should succeed. Third, Storehouse announced reduced profits for the half-year to September as a result of a disastrous performance by the new stock control system at Mothercare. On 15 November, the *Sunday Times* estimated that Benlox spoke for 0% of Storehouse shares.

Storehouse – update to mid-April 1988

1   The Benlox bid for Storehouse lapsed in December 1987 having attracted acceptances from less than 1% of shareholders. But Benlox maintained its claim of 3% support, saying that institutions had not bothered to accept once it was clear that support would be less than 50%.

2   In late 1987 and early 1988 some minor changes to Storehouse's business portfolio were made:

(a)   Blazer, a specialist retailer of six menswear shops in the London area, was bought. This complements the Storehouse investment in Anonymous, a specialised womenswear retailer also in London.

(b)   Loss-making stores in the Netherlands were sold to managers or converted to franchise, rather than wholly owned, operations.

(c)   Citibank's 50% holding in Storecard, the Storehouse credit card, was purchased for £2.2m.

3   Pre-tax profit forecasts for 1987/8 and 1988/9 have been steadily downgraded. Current company estimates are £113m and £130m respectively compared with earlier expectations of £135–140m for 1987/8 and an actual figure of £129m for 1986/7. These dismal projections led to share price underperformance until late April (see graph below).

4   The appointment of Michael Julian to the Chief Executive post in February indicated the beginning of the resolution of senior management difficulties. Julian is a financial expert with experience of major difficulties: at Guinness; at Midland Bank (with Crocker); and at Eurotunnel (with flotation difficulties). But his appointment does not take effect until June 1988.

5   Bid speculation revived in April. It was variously suggested that Lonrho, Robert Maxwell, Ashraf Marwan, Benlox's backer, and George Davies, Conran's former protégé at Next, were contemplating a bid. It is certain that Storehouse's share price moved ahead significantly and that Shearson Lehman, backers of the Mountleigh bid in August 1987, were openly circulating a 'battle plan' to potential bidders.

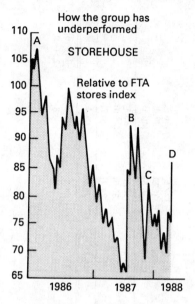

How the group has underperformed

STOREHOUSE

Relative to FTA stores index

Source: The Sunday Times, 24 April 1988

(A) Formation of Storehouse
(B) Mountleigh bid
(C) Benlox bid
(D) Renewed bid speculation

NB: This chart shows relative price levels. It cannot therefore show the impact of the stock market crash. The absolute price of Storehouse shares in early April was just over £2 compared with the Mountleigh cash offer of £4.50 in August 1987.

Appendix 17.1   *Habitat, Habitat-Mothercare, and Storehouse: Profit and Loss Account*

£m

Year to:	28 Jun 81	27 Jun 82(1)	27 Mar 83(2)	25 Mar 84	31 Mar 85	29 Mar 86(3)	4 Apr 87(4)	19 Sep 87(5)
Turnover	67.2	157.1	244.0	375.4	446.8	1057.8	1120.6	481.4(+4)
Earnings before interest and tax	5.5	11.0	22.5	36.2	43.0	122.6	136.6	
Interest	(1.1)	(1.0)	(3.2)	(5.6)	(6.5)	(6.5)	(7.4)	
Tax	(1.5)	(3.2)	(7.3)	(11.4)	(12.9)	(36.5)	(40.1)	
Earnings	2.9	6.8	12.0	19.2	23.6	79.6	89.1	
Dividends	(0.5)	(4.2)	(4.2)	(6.9)	(8.5)	(30.5)	(35.0)	
Extraordinary items (6)	(0.6)	0.1	3.0	(5.4)	1.1	(24.1)	(0.7)	
Retained earnings	1.8	2.7	10.8	6.9	16.2	25.0	53.4	
Eps (basic), pence	8.6	9.9	11.3	18.2	22.3	21.6	22.2	6.1(–5)
Dividend per share, pence		4.0	4.0	6.5	8.0	7.7	8.6	2.5(+9)

Notes

(1) Includes Mothercare from 14 Jan 82
(2) 39 weeks
(3) Although Storehouse was not formed until January 1986, the 1986 accounts show how Storehouse would have performed had it been in existence throughout the financial year
(4) 53 weeks. Turnover figures exclude £32.5m from discounted activities (Now and BHS food)
(5) Half year results (24 weeks). Figures in brackets show percentage changes over the same period in 1986/7
(6) There was an extraordinary tax charge of £4.5m in 1983/4 and charges of £24.1m in connection with closure of Now and BHS' food activities in 1985/6. Other extraordinary items are currency fluctuations

Appendix 17.2 *Habitat-Mothercare and Storehouse: Balance Sheets*[1]

£m

As at:	27 Jun 82	27 Mar 83	25 Mar 84	31 Mar 85	29 Mar 86	4 Apr 87
Fixed assets	96.7	112.2	127.3	151.5	401.8	503.1
Investments	2.7	2.0	16.7	15.6	57.7	38.9
	99.4	114.2	144.0	167.1	459.5	542.0
Stocks	49.1	67.0	68.7	82.4	161.5	182.7
Debtors	9.1	9.7	13.9	17.9	44.9	61.0
Cash	5.8	7.0	9.9	8.0	45.2	52.9
Creditors	(44.9)	(64.9)	(72.8)	(83.0)	(181.1)	(204.6)
Short-term loans	(7.1)	(9.5)	(12.4)	(16.3)	(46.7)	(52.2)
Net current assets	12.0	9.3	7.3	9.0	23.8	39.8
	111.4	123.5	151.3	176.1	483.3	581.8
Long-term loans[2]	40.0	43.2	61.5	71.2	50.6	102.7
Deferred tax	1.3	0.5	4.3	3.3	30.3	22.3
Share capital (10p ord)	41.3	43.7	65.8	74.5	80.9	125.0
Other shareholders' funds	10.6	10.6	10.6	10.6	39.8	40.4
	59.5	69.4	74.9	91.0	362.7	416.5
	111.4	123.5	151.3	176.1	483.3	581.8

Notes

(1) The first four are for Habitat-Mothercare, the last two for Storehouse
(2) Includes, in 1986, a provision of £12.6m against closure of BHS food activities

Appendix 17.3 *Habitat, Habitat-Mothercare, and Storehouse: Analysis of Turnover*

Year to:	28 Jun 81	27 Jun 82(1)	27 Mar 83(2)	25 Mar 84	31 Mar 85	29 Mar 86(3)	4 Apr 87(4)	19 Sep 87(5)
				£m				
Habitat	67.2	82.7	86.2	137.9	167.4	184.6	210.7	93.7 (+11)
Mothercare		74.4	157.8	237.5	279.4	292.3	306.4	132.2 (−4)
BHS						580.9(6)	533.9	224.3 (+7)
Richards(7)							37.1	n/a
	67.2	157.1	244.0	375.4	446.8	1057.8	1088.1	481.4 (+4)
UK	38.4	102.0	165.8	260.8	307.0	914.6	920.5	
Europe	22.1	35.4	43.8	56.1	64.6	69.5	88.6	
USA	6.6	19.8	34.4	58.5	75.1	73.7	79.0	
	67.1	157.2	244.0	375.4	446.7	1057.8	1088.1	

Notes

(1) Includes Mothercare from 14 Jan 82
(2) 39 weeks
(3) Although Storehouse was not formed until January 1986, the 1986 accounts show how Storehouse would have performed had it been in existence throughout the financial year
(4) 53 weeks. Turnover figures include £32.5m from discontinued activities (Now and BHS food)
(5) Half year results (24 weeks). Figures in brackets show percentage changes over the same period in 1986/7
(6) Includes £85m of food sales. Food sales were subsequently ended.
(7) Prior to 1987, Richards was treated as an associated company

Appendix 17.4 *Habitat, Habitat-Mothercare, and Storehouse: Analysis of Trading Profit*

£m

Year to:	28 Jun 81	27 Jun 82(1)	27 Mar 83(2)	25 Mar 84	31 Mar 85	29 Mar 86(3)	4 Apr 87(4)	19 Sep 87(5)
Habitat	5.3	6.3	7.3	9.9	11.2	13.2	14.5	4.4(+26)
Mothercare		4.9	15.5	25.3	32.7	38.4	34.9	9.9(−27)
BHS						59.8	70.7	20.0(+10)
SavaCentre, etc						} 4.2	9.3	n/a
Richards							3.9	n/a
Total(6)	**5.3**	**11.2**	**22.8**	**35.1**	**43.9**	**115.6**	**133.3**	**n/a**
UK	4.6	10.3	21.4	34.1	42.0	106.7	117.6	
Europe	1.2	2.3	1.9	0.5	1.8	2.0	3.4	
USA	(0.5)	(1.3)	(0.4)	0.6	0.1	2.7	3.0	
SavaCentre, etc						4.2	9.3	
Total(6)	**5.3**	**11.3**	**22.9**	**35.2**	**43.98**	**115.6**	**133.3**	

Notes

(1) Includes Mothercare from 14 Jan 82
(2) 39 weeks
(3) Although Storehouse was not formed until January 1986, the 1986 accounts show how Storehouse would have performed had it been in existence throughout the financial year
(4) 53 weeks. Turnover figures exclude £32.5m from discontinued activities (Now and BHS food)
(5) Half year results (24 weeks). Figures in brackets show percentage changes over the same period in 1986/7
(6) The totals shown here differ from the earnings before interest and tax figures shown elsewhere because they exclude profits or losses of related companies, profits from property sales and the cost of employee profit sharing schemes

Appendix 17.5 *Five year record*

	1982 £000	1983 £000	1984 £000	1985 £000	1986 £000
Turnover					
BHS	427,563	455,684	494,394	550,444	580,929
Habitat-Mothercare	255,361	309,695	375,410	446,733	476,917
Total Storehouse	682,924	765,379	869,804	997,177	1,057,846
Trading profit					
BHS	40,479	43,708	49,927	55,350	59,809
Habitat-Mothercare	20,625	27,461	35,173	44,005	51,635
Total Storehouse	61,104	71,169	85,100	99,355	111,444
Profit before taxation					
BHS	42,562	48,874	55,193	61,165	70,195
Habitat-Mothercare	18,468	22,947	30,617	36,533	45,908
Total Storehouse	61,030	71,821	85,810	97,698	116,066
Profit after taxation					
BHS	26,797	27,163	34,009	37,831	44,854
Habitat-Mothercare	12,004	14,916	19,224	23,637	34,743
Total Storehouse	38,801	42,079	53,233	61,468	79,562
Number of stores					
BHS	120	123	124	128	127
Habitat-Mothercare	481	506	521	546	584
Total Storehouse	601	629	645	674	711
Net selling space (in '000 sq.ft.)					
BHS	2,926	2,992	3,033	3,148	3,230
Habitat-Mothercare	1,864	2,120	2,318	2,454	2,816
Total Storehouse	4,790	5,112	5,351	5,602	6,046
Average number of employees					
BHS	25,239	25,260	24,085	24,354	23,428
Habitat-Mothercare	8,750	9,148	10,418	10,959	11,841
Total Storehouse	33,989	34,408	34,503	35,313	35,269
Number of full time equivalents					
BHS	14,655	14,891	14,291	14,296	13,781
Habitat-Mothercare	6,035	6,306	7,068	7,436	7,873
Total Storehouse	20,690	21,197	21,359	21,732	21,654

Notes
This five year record has been extracted from the published accounts of BHS and Habitat-Mothercare. The only adjustments made relate to the adjustments to the 1985 figures to reflect the changes in accounting policies (see Note 19) and the reclassification of the provision for employee participation schemes previously reported by BHS as part of trading profit.
Turnover excludes sales taxes.
Profits before and after tax include the Group's share of the results of related companies.
1982 and 1983 figures include Habitat Mothercare's pro-forma twelve month period to March.
1986 figures for Total Storehouse include the results of the Company (see Note 19).

Appendix 17.6   *Major UK Stores Companies: Most Recent Sales, Pre-tax Profits, P/E ratios and Market Capitalisations*

	Latest Accounts	Sales £m	Pre-tax Profit £m	As at 14 Dec 87 Mkt Cap	P/E
Ashley, L	Jan 87	171	22	227	17.4
Boots	Mar 87	2,352	243	2,081	13.0
Burton	Aug 86	1,229	149	1,228	10.3
Dixon	Apr 86	943	78	778	10.9
Marks & Spencer	Mar 87	3,735	366	4,838	17.9
Next	Aug 86	190	27	1,005	24.3
Sears	Jan 87	2,480	219	1,984	15.1
Smith, W H	May 87	1,527	64	509	15.5
Storehouse	Apr 87	1,121	129	1,020	12.3
Woolworth	Jan 87	1,828	115	1,111	n/a